PHARMACEUTICS

GUIDE TO DOSAGE FORMS AS PER PCI SYLLABUS FOR 1ST YEAR B.PHARMACY

MOUNIKA KUCHUKUNTLA, DR.RAJENDRA KUMAR JADI, DR.UPPU PAVANI

Made with ♥ on the Notion Press Platform
www.notionpress.com

Contents

Pharmaceutics

Guide to Dosage Forms as per PCI Syllabus for 1ˢᵗ Year B.Pharmacy

Mrs. Mounika Kuchukuntla

M. Pharm., (Ph.D)

Associate Professor, Department of Pharmaceutics

School of Pharmacy, Anurag University

Venkatapur, Ghatkesar, Medchal-Malkajgiri

Hyderabad - 500 088, Telangana, India.

Dr. Rajendra Kumar Jadi

M. Pharm., Ph.D

Associate Professor, Department of Pharmaceutics

School of Pharmacy, Anurag University

Venkatapur, Ghatkesar, Medchal-Malkajgiri

Hyderabad - 500 088, Telangana, India.

Dr. Uppu Pavani

M. Pharm., Ph.D

Associate Professor, Head - Department of Pharmaceutics

Nethaji Institute of Pharmaceutical Sciences

Somidi, Kazipet, Warangal

Telangana - 506009, India.

Published by Notion Press

Notion Press, Inc.

800, West El Camino Real #180,

California, USA 94040

Notion Press Media Pvt Ltd,

#7, Red Cross Road,

Egmore, Chennai, Tamil Nadu 600008

Email ID: publish@notionpress.com

Phone Number: +91 44 46315631

CHAPTER ONE

Historical Background and Development of the Profession of Pharmacy

Early History of Pharmacy

The origins of pharmacy can be traced back to ancient civilizations, where the roles of healer, priest, and pharmacist were often intertwined. In **Mesopotamia**, around 2600 BC, the earliest records of pharmacy practice were found on clay tablets. These tablets contained lists of prescriptions, instructions for compounding, and the names of medicinal plants. The Sumerians and Babylonians were known to prepare medicines by grinding plants, mixing them with water, and storing them in clay pots.

In **Ancient Egypt**, pharmacy was closely linked with religion. The Ebers Papyrus, dating back to around 1550 BC, is one of the oldest and most important medical documents. It contains over 800 prescriptions using around 700 drugs, including plants, minerals, and animal products. Egyptian pharmacists, often priests, prepared these medications in temple laboratories. Their methods were highly advanced for their time, including techniques like extraction, filtration, and the preparation of pills and ointments.

Greek contributions to pharmacy were significant, especially between the 5th and 4th centuries BC. Hippocrates, known as the "Father of Medicine," emphasized the importance of diet and lifestyle in health and introduced the concept of the four humors. Theophrastus, a student of Aristotle, is often called the "Father of Botany" for his extensive studies on plants and their medicinal uses. Another notable figure, Dioscorides, wrote "De Materia Medica," a comprehensive text on medicinal substances used for over 1500 years.

In **Ancient China**, pharmacy developed through the practice of traditional Chinese medicine. The Shennong Ben Cao Jing, attributed to the legendary emperor Shennong, categorized 365 species of medicinal plants. This text laid the foundation for Chinese herbal medicine, which remains influential today. Chinese pharmacists, often part of the medical practice, utilized plants, minerals, and animal products to create complex remedies.

The **Islamic Golden Age** saw significant advancements in pharmacy between the 8th and 14th centuries. Scholars like Avicenna (Ibn Sina) wrote comprehensive texts that combined the knowledge of Greek, Roman, and Persian medicine. His "Canon of Medicine" included detailed descriptions of drugs and their effects. Islamic pharmacists, or saydalani, established the first apothecaries, which were early versions of modern pharmacies.

India has a rich history of pharmacy, deeply rooted in its ancient medicinal systems, particularly **Ayurveda**. Dating back to around 3000 BC, Ayurveda is one of the world's oldest holistic healing systems. Ancient texts such as the Charaka Samhita and Sushruta Samhita detailed the use of numerous medicinal plants, minerals, and animal products. These texts provided extensive knowledge on the preparation, properties, and uses of various drugs. The practice of Rasashastra, the Ayurvedic science of alchemy, contributed significantly to the development of pharmaceuticals, including the use of metals and minerals in medicine. The establishment of traditional medicine systems like Ayurveda, Siddha, and Unani in India laid the foundation for a comprehensive approach to health and disease management. These traditional systems continue to influence modern pharmacy practices in India and around the world.

In **medieval Europe**, the preservation and expansion of pharmaceutical knowledge were largely due to monastic communities. Monks in monasteries grew medicinal plants and prepared remedies, compiling their knowledge in texts called herbals. The establishment of universities in the 12th century further formalized the education of pharmacists and physicians.

By the **Renaissance**, the separation of pharmacy from medicine began to take shape. Pharmacists, known as apothecaries, started to form guilds and associations to regulate the practice and ensure the quality of medicines. The development of pharmacopoeias, official lists of medicinal substances and their preparation methods, provided standardized guidelines for the profession.

The early history of pharmacy is marked by a continuous evolution of knowledge and practices. Each civilization contributed unique insights and techniques, laying the groundwork for modern pharmacy. The meticulous documentation and use of natural substances by early pharmacists reflect the enduring commitment to improving health and treating diseases

Development in Different Civilizations

The development of pharmacy has been significantly influenced by various civilizations, each contributing unique practices, knowledge, and advancements. These contributions have collectively shaped the profession into what it is today.

Mesopotamia: In ancient Mesopotamia, pharmacy began as a component of the broader medical practices carried out by asu (physicians) and asipu (exorcists). As early as 2600 BC, clay tablets recorded the preparation of medicines, including detailed descriptions of ingredients and methods. Mesopotamian pharmacists used natural products such as plants, minerals, and animal parts, often in conjunction with spiritual rituals. The Code of Hammurabi, a set of laws from around 1750 BC, included regulations for medical practitioners, indicating an early recognition of the need for professional standards in healthcare.

Egypt: Ancient Egyptian pharmacy was highly advanced, with significant integration into religious practices. The Ebers Papyrus, dating back to around 1550 BC, provides a comprehensive look at Egyptian medicinal practices. It lists hundreds of remedies for a variety of ailments, showcasing the Egyptians' extensive use of botanical, mineral, and animal substances. Egyptian pharmacists, who often worked in temples, developed sophisticated methods for preparing medications, including extraction, infusion, and compounding. Their approach combined empirical knowledge with spiritual beliefs, aiming to treat both the body and the soul.

Greece: The Greek civilization made profound contributions to the field of pharmacy. Around the 5th and 4th centuries BC, Hippocrates laid the groundwork for scientific medicine, emphasizing natural causes of diseases and advocating for dietary and lifestyle interventions. Theophrastus, a student of Aristotle, is often regarded as the "Father of Botany" for his detailed studies on medicinal plants. His works laid the foundation for the systematic study of botany and pharmacology. Dioscorides, a Greek physician in the 1ˢᵗ century AD, wrote "De Materia Medica," an extensive pharmacopeia that cataloged hundreds of medicinal substances, including their uses, dosages, and preparations. This work remained a standard reference for over a millennium.

China: In ancient China, the development of pharmacy was closely linked to traditional Chinese medicine. The Shennong Ben Cao Jing, attributed to the legendary emperor Shennong, categorized 365 medicinal plants and provided guidelines for their use. This text, dating back to around 2000 BC, formed the basis for Chinese herbal medicine. Chinese pharmacists employed a holistic approach, combining plant, mineral, and animal products to create complex remedies tailored to individual patients. The practice emphasized balance and harmony within the body, principles that are still central to traditional Chinese medicine today.

India: India has a rich history of pharmacy, deeply rooted in its ancient medicinal systems, particularly Ayurveda. Dating back to around 3000 BC, Ayurveda is one of the world's oldest holistic healing systems. Ancient texts such as the Charaka Samhita and Sushruta Samhita detailed the use of numerous medicinal plants, minerals, and animal products. These texts provided extensive knowledge on the preparation, properties, and uses of various drugs. The practice of Rasashastra, the Ayurvedic science of alchemy, contributed significantly to the development of pharmaceuticals, including the use of metals and minerals in medicine. The establishment of traditional medicine systems like Ayurveda, Siddha, and Unani in India laid the foundation for a comprehensive approach to health and disease management. These traditional systems continue to influence modern pharmacy practices in India and around the world.

Islamic Civilization: During the Islamic Golden Age (8ᵗʰ to 14ᵗʰ centuries), pharmacy saw significant advancements due to the synthesis of Greek, Roman, Persian, and Indian knowledge. Islamic scholars such as Avicenna (Ibn Sina) and Al-Razi (Rhazes) wrote extensively on medicine and pharmacology. Avicenna's "Canon of Medicine" included detailed descriptions of hundreds of drugs, their properties, and therapeutic uses. Islamic pharmacists, known as saydalani, established the first apothecaries, where they compounded and dispensed medicines. These early pharmacies adhered to strict standards, ensuring the quality and purity of their products. The Islamic world also saw the introduction of new medicinal substances and advanced techniques for drug preparation and storage.

Medieval Europe: In medieval Europe, the knowledge of pharmacy was preserved and expanded by monastic communities. Monks in monasteries cultivated medicinal plants and compiled their knowledge in herbals, detailed manuscripts that described the uses and preparation of various remedies. The establishment of universities in the 12th century marked the formalization of pharmacy education. Universities such as the University of Salerno in Italy included pharmacy in their medical curriculum, training students in the art and science of compounding medicines. During this period, the separation of pharmacy from medicine began to take shape, with apothecaries emerging as distinct professionals responsible for preparing and dispensing medications.

Renaissance and Beyond: The Renaissance period witnessed significant advancements in pharmacy. The publication of pharmacopoeias, official compendia listing standardized drugs and their preparations, marked a major step towards modern pharmacy. The first pharmacopoeia, "Pharmacopoeia Augustana," was published in Augsburg, Germany, in 1564. This era also saw the establishment of guilds and associations for apothecaries, which regulated the profession and ensured the quality of medicinal products. The scientific revolution of the 17th and 18th centuries further propelled the field, with discoveries in chemistry and biology leading to the development of new drugs and therapeutic practices.

In summary, the development of pharmacy across different civilizations highlights the diverse approaches and innovations that have shaped the profession. From the empirical practices of Mesopotamia and Egypt to the scientific advancements of Greece, China, India, the Islamic world, and medieval Europe, each civilization contributed to the evolution of pharmacy. These historical developments laid the foundation for modern pharmacy, characterized by rigorous scientific research, standardized practices, and a commitment to improving public health.

History of Pharmacy in India

Ancient to Modern Pharmacy in India

The history of pharmacy in India is deeply intertwined with the country's ancient medicinal practices and has evolved significantly over the millennia.

Ancient Period: In ancient India, pharmacy was a vital component of **Ayurveda**, the traditional system of medicine that dates back to around

3000 BC. Ayurvedic texts such as the **Charaka Samhita** and **Sushruta Samhita** are among the oldest comprehensive medical documents. These texts describe the properties, preparation, and uses of numerous medicinal plants, minerals, and animal products. The **Charaka Samhita** focuses on internal medicine and details the preparation of complex herbal formulations, while the **Sushruta Samhita** provides extensive insights into surgery and the use of medicinal compounds for post-operative care.

The practice of **Rasashastra**, an Ayurvedic branch focusing on the use of metals and minerals, further advanced the field of pharmacy. Alchemists, known as **Rasa Vaidyas**, developed sophisticated techniques for purifying and preparing substances like mercury, gold, and sulfur, which were believed to have potent therapeutic properties. These practices laid the groundwork for the development of pharmaceutical chemistry in India.

Medieval Period: During the medieval period, the influence of **Unani** medicine, introduced by the Persians and further developed under Mughal rule, became prominent. Unani medicine integrated with existing Ayurvedic practices, leading to a rich, syncretic tradition of pharmacy in India. Unani texts such as the **Tibb-e-Akbar** and **Makhzan al-Adwiya** documented a vast array of medicinal substances and their formulations, contributing to the diversity of Indian pharmacy.

The medieval period also saw the establishment of **madrasas** and **hospitals** that served as centers for medical education and pharmaceutical practice. These institutions preserved and expanded the knowledge of both Ayurvedic and Unani systems, ensuring the continued development of pharmacy in India.

Colonial Period: The colonial era marked a significant shift in Indian pharmacy. The introduction of Western medicine by British colonizers led to the establishment of the first modern pharmacies and pharmaceutical companies. The **Bengal Chemical and Pharmaceutical Works (BCPW)**, founded by Acharya Prafulla Chandra Ray in 1901, was the first Indian-owned pharmaceutical company, pioneering the production of chemicals and medicines locally.

In 1932, the **University of Calcutta** introduced the first Bachelor of Pharmacy (B.Pharm) program, laying the foundation for formal pharmacy education in India. The establishment of the **Pharmacy Act** in 1948 and the formation of the **Pharmacy Council of India (PCI)** standardized pharmacy education and practice, ensuring the quality and professionalism of pharmacists across the country.

Post-Independence Period: Following India's independence in 1947, the pharmaceutical industry experienced rapid growth. The government established public sector enterprises such as **Hindustan Antibiotics Limited (HAL)** in 1954 and **Indian Drugs and Pharmaceuticals Limited (IDPL)** in 1961 to reduce dependence on imported drugs and promote self-sufficiency.

The **Indian Patent Act** of 1970, which allowed the production of generic drugs, catalyzed the growth of the domestic pharmaceutical industry. Indian companies such as **Cipla, Ranbaxy**, and **Dr. Reddy's Laboratories** emerged as significant players in the global market, known for producing affordable and high-quality generic medicines.

Modern Era: In recent decades, India has become a global hub for pharmaceuticals, known as the "pharmacy of the world." The country is one of the largest producers of generic drugs and vaccines, supplying over 50% of global demand for various vaccines. Indian pharmaceutical companies have expanded their research and development capabilities, focusing on innovative drug formulations and biotechnology.

The establishment of institutions like the **National Institute of Pharmaceutical Education and Research (NIPER)** has further advanced pharmaceutical education and research in India. NIPER and other leading universities offer advanced programs in pharmaceutical sciences, fostering a new generation of skilled pharmacists and researchers.

Today, the Indian pharmaceutical industry is a critical component of the global healthcare system, renowned for its contributions to public health through the development and distribution of essential medicines. The integration of traditional practices with modern scientific advancements continues to drive the evolution of pharmacy in India, reflecting the country's rich heritage and innovative spirit.

Key Milestones in Indian Pharmacy

The history of pharmacy in India is marked by numerous significant milestones that have shaped its development from ancient times to the modern era. These milestones reflect the evolution of pharmaceutical practices, education, industry, and regulation in India.

Ancient Period:

- **3000 BC: Development of Ayurveda** - Ayurveda, one of the world's oldest holistic healing systems, lays the foundation for Indian pharmacy. Texts like the **Charaka Samhita** and **Sushruta Samhita** document the use of medicinal plants, minerals, and animal products.
- **2000 BC: Rasashastra** - The science of alchemy and the use of metals in medicine begin, contributing significantly to pharmaceutical chemistry.

Medieval Period:

- **13th Century: Integration of Unani Medicine** - Persian and Mughal influences introduce Unani medicine to India, enriching the pharmaceutical traditions with new medicinal substances and formulations.
- **15th Century: Madrasas and Hospitals** - Establishment of educational institutions and hospitals that serve as centers for medical and pharmaceutical knowledge.

Colonial Period:

- **1901: Founding of Bengal Chemical and Pharmaceutical Works (BCPW)** - Acharya Prafulla Chandra Ray establishes India's first pharmaceutical company, pioneering the local production of chemicals and medicines.
- **1932: Introduction of B.Pharm Program at University of Calcutta** - The first formal pharmacy education program in India is introduced, laying the foundation for professional training in pharmacy.
- **1948: Enactment of the Pharmacy Act** - The Pharmacy Act is established to regulate pharmacy education and practice, leading to the formation of the Pharmacy Council of India (PCI).

Post-Independence Period:

- **1954: Establishment of Hindustan Antibiotics Limited (HAL)** - The government sets up HAL to reduce dependence on imported antibiotics and promote self-sufficiency.
- **1961: Establishment of Indian Drugs and Pharmaceuticals Limited (IDPL)** - IDPL is founded to boost the production of essential drugs and support the growth of the domestic pharmaceutical industry.

- **1970**: **Indian Patent Act** - The Act abolishes product patents for pharmaceuticals, allowing Indian companies to produce generic versions of patented drugs, significantly lowering drug costs and increasing accessibility.
- **1988**: **Formation of the Indian Pharmaceutical Association (IPA)** - The IPA is established to promote the interests of pharmacists and the pharmaceutical profession in India.

Modern Era:

- **1998**: **Establishment of National Institute of Pharmaceutical Education and Research (NIPER)** - NIPER is established to advance pharmaceutical education and research, becoming a premier institution for training and innovation.
- **2000s**: **Expansion of Indian Pharmaceutical Industry** - Indian companies like **Cipla**, **Ranbaxy**, **Dr. Reddy's Laboratories**, and **Sun Pharma** emerge as global leaders in the production of generic drugs and active pharmaceutical ingredients (APIs).
- **2010s**: **India as a Global Pharmaceutical Hub** - India becomes one of the largest producers of generic drugs and vaccines, supplying a significant portion of the global demand. The country also excels in contract research and manufacturing services (CRAMS).
- **2020s**: **COVID-19 Pandemic Response** - Indian pharmaceutical companies play a crucial role in the global response to the COVID-19 pandemic, producing and supplying essential drugs, vaccines, and medical supplies.

These key milestones highlight the dynamic and progressive nature of the pharmacy profession in India. From ancient traditions to modern innovations, India's contributions to pharmacy have had a profound impact on global health and continue to drive advancements in the field.

Evolution of Pharmacy Education and Industry

Development of Pharmacy Education

The development of pharmacy education in India has evolved significantly over the years, reflecting the growing importance of the pharmaceutical profession in healthcare. The journey from traditional knowledge systems to modern scientific education has been marked by key milestones and progressive advancements.

Ancient and Medieval Periods: Pharmacy education in India can be traced back to the ancient systems of **Ayurveda** and **Unani** medicine. **Ayurvedic** texts such as the **Charaka Samhita** and **Sushruta Samhita** not only documented medicinal practices but also served as educational material for aspiring physicians and pharmacists. **Gurukuls**, traditional Hindu educational institutions, provided training in Ayurveda, where students learned about medicinal plants, formulations, and therapeutic techniques under the guidance of experienced practitioners.

During the **medieval period**, the integration of **Unani** medicine further enriched pharmaceutical education. Madrasas, Islamic educational institutions, played a crucial role in imparting knowledge of Unani medicine. These institutions provided comprehensive training in the preparation and use of medicinal substances, drawing from Greek, Persian, and Indian traditions.

Colonial Period: The introduction of Western medicine by British colonizers brought significant changes to pharmacy education in India. In 1892, the **University of Madras** established a pharmacy course, marking the beginning of formal pharmacy education in the country. However, it was the establishment of the **Bengal Chemical and Pharmaceutical Works (BCPW)** by Acharya Prafulla Chandra Ray in 1901 that truly laid the foundation for professional pharmacy practice and education.

In 1932, the **University of Calcutta** introduced the first **Bachelor of Pharmacy (B.Pharm)** program, providing structured education in pharmaceutical sciences. This program included subjects such as pharmacology, medicinal chemistry, and pharmaceutics, equipping students with scientific knowledge and practical skills.

Post-Independence Period: Following India's independence in 1947, there was a concerted effort to standardize and enhance pharmacy education. The enactment of the **Pharmacy Act of 1948** was a landmark development, leading to the formation of the **Pharmacy Council of India (PCI)**. The PCI was established to regulate pharmacy education and practice, ensuring uniform standards across the country. It mandated the introduction of diploma (D.Pharm) and degree (B.Pharm) courses in pharmacy, along with standardized curricula and examinations.

The 1950s and 1960s saw the establishment of several pharmacy colleges and universities offering B.Pharm programs. These institutions focused on providing comprehensive education in pharmaceutical sciences, including pharmacology, pharmacognosy, pharmaceutical chemistry, and pharmaceutics. The introduction of the **Master of Pharmacy (M.Pharm)** and **Doctor of Philosophy (Ph.D.)** programs further advanced pharmacy education, promoting research and specialization in various fields of pharmacy.

Modern Era: In the late 20th and early 21st centuries, pharmacy education in India underwent significant transformation to align with global standards. The establishment of the **National Institute of Pharmaceutical Education and Research (NIPER)** in 1998 marked a major milestone. NIPER was set up as a premier institution for higher education and research in pharmaceutical sciences, offering advanced programs such as M.Pharm, Ph.D., and integrated Ph.D. courses. It aimed to produce highly skilled professionals and researchers capable of contributing to the global pharmaceutical industry.

The introduction of the **Doctor of Pharmacy (Pharm.D)** program in 2008 represented another significant advancement. The Pharm.D program, a six-year course including five years of academic study and one year of internship, was designed to produce clinical pharmacists with expertise in patient care, clinical research, and therapeutic management. This program emphasized the role of pharmacists in healthcare teams, improving patient outcomes through effective medication management and counseling.

Technological Integration and Contemporary Trends: In recent years, the integration of technology into pharmacy education has been a key trend. Online learning platforms, virtual labs, and digital resources have enhanced the accessibility and quality of pharmacy education. Institutions have adopted innovative teaching methods, including simulation-based learning and interprofessional education, to prepare students for the evolving demands of the healthcare industry.

The focus on research and development has also intensified, with pharmacy colleges and universities establishing state-of-the-art laboratories and research centers. Collaborative research projects, industry partnerships, and international collaborations have become integral to pharmacy education, promoting innovation and knowledge exchange.

Challenges and Future Directions: Despite significant progress, pharmacy education in India faces challenges such as the need for updated curricula, faculty development, and infrastructure improvements. Addressing these challenges requires continuous efforts from educational institutions, regulatory bodies, and the government.

Looking ahead, the future of pharmacy education in India is promising, with an emphasis on interdisciplinary education, personalized medicine, and the integration of artificial intelligence and data analytics. The evolving healthcare landscape demands pharmacists who are not only knowledgeable in pharmaceutical sciences but also skilled in patient care, research, and technology.

In conclusion, the development of pharmacy education in India reflects a rich history of traditional knowledge and modern advancements. From ancient Ayurveda and Unani systems to contemporary scientific education, pharmacy education in India has evolved to meet the needs of society and the healthcare industry. As the field continues to advance, pharmacy education will play a crucial role in shaping the future of healthcare, ensuring the provision of safe, effective, and affordable medicines to the population.

Evolution of Pharmacy Education and Industry

Growth of the Pharmaceutical Industry

The growth of the pharmaceutical industry in India has been remarkable, transforming from a nascent sector into a global powerhouse. This evolution can be traced through several key phases, each marked by significant developments and contributions.

Early Foundations: The foundation of the Indian pharmaceutical industry was laid during the late 19th and early 20th centuries. In 1901, **Acharya Prafulla Chandra Ray** established the **Bengal Chemical and Pharmaceutical Works (BCPW)** in Kolkata, marking the beginning of the Indian pharmaceutical sector. BCPW was the first Indian-owned company to manufacture pharmaceuticals, chemicals, and indigenous medicines. This initiative was a significant step towards self-reliance in the production of medicines.

Post-Independence Era: Following India's independence in 1947, the government recognized the importance of developing a robust pharmaceutical industry to ensure the availability of essential medicines. The establishment of public sector enterprises played a crucial role in this regard. In 1954, the government set up **Hindustan Antibiotics Limited (HAL),** the first public sector pharmaceutical company, aimed at reducing dependency on imported antibiotics. This was followed by the establishment of **Indian Drugs and Pharmaceuticals Limited (IDPL)** in 1961, which further strengthened the domestic production of essential drugs.

Indian Patent Act of 1970: A pivotal moment in the growth of the Indian pharmaceutical industry was the enactment of the **Indian Patent Act of 1970**. This legislation abolished product patents for pharmaceuticals, allowing Indian companies to produce generic versions of patented drugs through process patents. This led to a surge in the production of affordable generic medicines, making healthcare more accessible to the Indian population. Companies like **Cipla**, **Ranbaxy Laboratories**, **Dr. Reddy's Laboratories**, and **Sun Pharmaceuticals** emerged as key players during this period, focusing on the development and manufacturing of high-quality generic drugs.

1980s and 1990s: Expansion and Global Reach: The 1980s and 1990s witnessed significant expansion of the Indian pharmaceutical industry, driven by increased investment in research and development (R&D) and the adoption of advanced manufacturing technologies. Indian pharmaceutical companies began to export their products to international markets, establishing a global presence. The focus on quality and compliance with international regulatory standards enabled Indian companies to gain a foothold in highly regulated markets such as the United States and Europe.

1990s and Early 2000s: Research and Innovation: The late 1990s and early 2000s saw Indian pharmaceutical companies investing heavily in R&D to move up the value chain from generic manufacturing to drug discovery and innovation. The establishment of the **National Institute of Pharmaceutical Education and Research (NIPER)** in 1998 provided a significant boost to pharmaceutical education and research in India. NIPER and other leading institutions fostered collaboration between academia and industry, promoting innovation in drug development.

During this period, Indian pharmaceutical companies began to focus on developing new chemical entities (NCEs) and novel drug delivery systems (NDDS). Collaborative research projects with international pharmaceutical companies and research institutions became common, enhancing the capabilities of Indian companies in cutting-edge pharmaceutical research.

Present Day: A Global Pharmaceutical Hub: Today, India is known as the "pharmacy of the world," being one of the largest producers of generic drugs and active pharmaceutical ingredients (APIs). The Indian pharmaceutical industry plays a critical role in global healthcare, supplying over 50% of the world's demand for various vaccines, 40% of the generic demand in the United States, and 25% of all medicines in the United Kingdom.

Indian pharmaceutical companies continue to expand their global footprint through mergers and acquisitions, strategic partnerships, and the establishment of manufacturing facilities abroad. The focus on biopharmaceuticals, biotechnology, and biosimilars represents the next frontier for the Indian pharmaceutical industry, with companies like **Biocon** leading the way in developing biosimilar products for global markets.

COVID-19 Pandemic Response: The COVID-19 pandemic underscored the critical role of the Indian pharmaceutical industry in global healthcare. Indian companies ramped up the production of essential medicines, vaccines, and medical supplies to meet the unprecedented demand. **Serum Institute of India**, the world's largest vaccine manufacturer, played a pivotal role in producing and supplying COVID-19 vaccines, both domestically and internationally. The collaboration between Indian pharmaceutical companies and global organizations, such as the World Health Organization (WHO) and Gavi, the Vaccine Alliance, highlighted India's capacity to respond to global health crises effectively.

Future Directions: The future of the Indian pharmaceutical industry looks promising, with several trends shaping its growth trajectory:

1. **Innovation and R&D**: Continued investment in R&D to develop new drugs, biologics, and advanced therapeutic modalities.
2. **Digital Transformation**: Adoption of digital technologies, including artificial intelligence (AI) and machine learning (ML), to enhance drug discovery, manufacturing, and supply chain management.
3. **Regulatory Compliance**: Strengthening regulatory frameworks to ensure the highest standards of quality and safety for pharmaceutical products.
4. **Sustainability**: Focus on sustainable manufacturing practices to minimize environmental impact and promote green chemistry.
5. **Healthcare Accessibility**: Enhancing access to affordable medicines and healthcare services, particularly in low- and middle-income countries.

The growth of the pharmaceutical industry in India has been marked by significant milestones that have transformed it into a global leader in the production of affordable, high-quality medicines. From its early foundations to its current status as a pharmaceutical hub, the industry continues to innovate and expand, contributing to global health and well-being.

National and International Organizations

Pharmacy organizations play a crucial role in regulating the profession, setting standards, promoting research, and ensuring the continuous professional development of pharmacists. These organizations operate at both national and international levels, contributing significantly to the advancement of pharmaceutical sciences and the healthcare industry.

National Organizations

1. **Pharmacy Council of India (PCI)**

   - **Role**: The PCI is a statutory body established under the Pharmacy Act of 1948. It regulates pharmacy education and practice in India, ensuring that standards are maintained across all institutions offering pharmacy courses.
   - **Functions**:

     - Prescribes minimum standards of education required for qualification as a pharmacist.
     - Conducts inspections of pharmacy institutions.
     - Approves pharmacy programs and institutions.
     - Registers pharmacists and maintains the central register of pharmacists.

1. **Indian Pharmaceutical Association (IPA)**

   - **Role**: The IPA is a professional association representing pharmacists across various sectors, including community, hospital, industry, and academia.
   - **Functions**:

     - Promotes the professional development of pharmacists through continuing education programs.

- Organizes conferences, seminars, and workshops to facilitate knowledge exchange.
- Publishes journals and newsletters to disseminate information on the latest developments in the field.
- Advocates for policy changes to improve the pharmacy profession and healthcare delivery.

3. **All India Organization of Chemists and Druggists (AIOCD)**

- **Role**: AIOCD is a trade organization representing the interests of retail and wholesale pharmacists in India.
- **Functions**:

  - Negotiates with the government and pharmaceutical companies on issues related to drug pricing and distribution.
  - Ensures the availability of medicines across the country.
  - Provides support and resources to its members to help them comply with regulatory requirements.

4. **National Institute of Pharmaceutical Education and Research (NIPER)**

- **Role**: NIPER is an autonomous institute under the Department of Pharmaceuticals, Government of India, established to promote high-quality education and research in pharmaceutical sciences.
- **Functions**:

  - Offers postgraduate and doctoral programs in various disciplines of pharmaceutical sciences.
  - Conducts cutting-edge research in drug discovery, development, and delivery.
  - Collaborates with industry and academic institutions to advance pharmaceutical education and innovation.

International Organizations

1. **International Pharmaceutical Federation (FIP)**

- **Role**: FIP is a global federation representing pharmacists and pharmaceutical scientists worldwide. It aims to improve global health by advancing pharmacy practice and science.
- **Functions**:

  - Sets international standards for pharmacy education and practice.
  - Organizes world congresses and conferences to foster global collaboration and knowledge exchange.
  - Publishes guidelines and position statements on various aspects of pharmacy and healthcare.
  - Engages with the World Health Organization (WHO) and other international bodies to influence global health policies.

2. **World Health Organization (WHO)**

- **Role**: WHO is a specialized agency of the United Nations responsible for international public health. It collaborates with member states and international organizations to promote health and well-being.
- **Functions**:

  - Develops guidelines and standards for the quality, safety, and efficacy of medicines.
  - Supports countries in strengthening their health systems and pharmaceutical sectors.
  - Conducts research and provides technical assistance on public health issues.
  - Monitors and evaluates global health trends and challenges.

3. **United States Pharmacopeia (USP)**

- **Role**: USP is a scientific non-profit organization that sets standards for the quality, purity, strength, and consistency of medicines, food ingredients, and dietary supplements.
- **Functions**:

  - Develops and publishes the United States Pharmacopeia and the National Formulary (USP-NF).

- Provides reference standards and tools for quality assurance in pharmaceuticals.
- Conducts training and education programs to support the implementation of USP standards.
- Collaborates with regulatory authorities, industry, and academia to enhance public health.

4. **European Directorate for the Quality of Medicines & HealthCare (EDQM)**

- **Role**: EDQM is a directorate of the Council of Europe responsible for the quality and safety of medicines and healthcare.
- **Functions**:

  - Develops and publishes the European Pharmacopoeia, setting quality standards for medicines in Europe.
  - Inspects and certifies pharmaceutical manufacturers to ensure compliance with quality standards.
  - Provides guidance and support to member states on regulatory and healthcare issues.
  - Promotes harmonization of pharmaceutical standards globally.

These national and international organizations are integral to the development and regulation of the pharmacy profession. They ensure that pharmacists are well-trained, medications are safe and effective, and that the public has access to high-quality healthcare services. Through their efforts, these organizations contribute to the continuous advancement of pharmaceutical sciences and the improvement of global health.

Roles and Contributions

Pharmacy organizations, both national and international, play pivotal roles in advancing the profession of pharmacy. Their contributions are critical in setting standards, promoting education, fostering research, advocating for policies, and ensuring public health and safety. Here's an overview of the roles and contributions of these organizations:

National Organizations

1. **Pharmacy Council of India (PCI)**

   - **Roles:**

     - Regulates pharmacy education and profession in India.
     - Ensures uniform standards of education across pharmacy institutions.
     - Maintains a central register of pharmacists.

   - **Contributions**:

     - Developed and implemented the pharmacy curriculum for diploma, degree, and postgraduate programs.
     - Conducts inspections and audits of pharmacy colleges to maintain educational quality.
     - Sets regulations and guidelines for the registration and practice of pharmacists in India.

2. **Indian Pharmaceutical Association (IPA)**

   - **Roles:**

     - Represents pharmacists in various sectors including community, hospital, industry, and academia.
     - Provides a platform for professional development and networking.

   - **Contributions:**

     - Organizes conferences, workshops, and continuing education programs to update pharmacists on the latest advancements and practices.
     - Publishes journals and newsletters that disseminate current research, news, and trends in pharmacy.
     - Advocates for policy changes to improve the pharmaceutical profession and healthcare delivery in India.

3. **All India Organization of Chemists and Druggists (AIOCD)**

- **Roles:**

  - Represents the interests of retail and wholesale pharmacists.
  - Ensures the availability and distribution of medicines.

- **Contributions:**

  - Negotiates with government and pharmaceutical companies on issues such as drug pricing and supply chain logistics.
  - Provides support to its members to ensure compliance with regulatory requirements.
  - Works to prevent the sale of counterfeit drugs and ensure the integrity of the pharmaceutical supply chain.

4. **National Institute of Pharmaceutical Education and Research (NIPER)**

   - **Roles:**

     - Promotes high-quality education and research in pharmaceutical sciences.
     - Collaborates with industry and academia to advance pharmaceutical education and innovation.

   - **Contributions:**

     - Offers postgraduate and doctoral programs that train the next generation of pharmaceutical scientists and professionals.
     - Conducts cutting-edge research in areas such as drug discovery, development, and delivery.
     - Establishes partnerships with international institutions to facilitate knowledge exchange and collaborative research projects.

International Organizations

1. **International Pharmaceutical Federation (FIP)**

   - **Roles:**

- Represents pharmacists and pharmaceutical scientists worldwide.
- Advocates for the advancement of the pharmaceutical sciences and practice.

- **Contributions**:

  - Sets international standards for pharmacy education and practice.
  - Organizes world congresses and conferences to promote global collaboration and knowledge exchange.
  - Publishes guidelines, position statements, and scientific papers on various aspects of pharmacy and healthcare.
  - Engages with WHO and other international bodies to influence global health policies.

2. **World Health Organization (WHO)**

- **Roles**:

  - Ensures global public health and safety.
  - Develops international guidelines and standards for medicines and healthcare.

- **Contributions**:

  - Provides leadership on global health matters and coordinates international responses to health emergencies.
  - Develops and publishes the WHO Model List of Essential Medicines, guiding countries on the most effective and safe medicines needed in a health system.
  - Conducts research and provides technical support to countries in strengthening their health systems and pharmaceutical sectors.
  - Monitors and evaluates global health trends, challenges, and progress.

3. **United States Pharmacopeia (USP)**

- **Roles**:

- Sets standards for the quality, purity, strength, and consistency of medicines, food ingredients, and dietary supplements.

- **Contributions:**

  - Develops and publishes the USP-NF (United States Pharmacopcia and National Formulary), which is recognized globally.
  - Provides reference standards and tools for quality assurance in pharmaceuticals.
  - Conducts training and education programs to support the implementation of USP standards worldwide.
  - Collaborates with regulatory authorities, industry, and academia to enhance public health.

4. **European Directorate for the Quality of Medicines & HealthCare (EDQM)**

  - **Roles:**

    - Ensures the quality and safety of medicines and healthcare in Europe.
    - Harmonizes pharmaceutical standards across Europe.

  - **Contributions:**

    - Develops and publishes the European Pharmacopoeia, setting quality standards for medicines in Europe.
    - Inspects and certifies pharmaceutical manufacturers to ensure compliance with quality standards.
    - Provides guidance and support to member states on regulatory and healthcare issues.
    - Promotes the harmonization of pharmaceutical standards globally, facilitating international trade and ensuring the quality of medicines.

Overall Contributions:

- **Regulation and Standardization**: Pharmacy organizations establish regulations and standards that ensure the quality, safety, and efficacy of pharmaceutical products and practices.
- **Education and Training**: They provide education and training programs that enhance the knowledge and skills of pharmacists, ensuring they are well-prepared to meet the needs of the healthcare system.
- **Research and Development**: By promoting and funding research, these organizations contribute to the discovery of new drugs, therapies, and pharmaceutical technologies.
- **Advocacy and Policy**: They advocate for policies that support the pharmacy profession and improve public health outcomes, engaging with governments, regulatory bodies, and other stakeholders.
- **Public Health and Safety**: Through their work, pharmacy organizations play a critical role in safeguarding public health by ensuring the availability of high-quality medicines and promoting the rational use of drugs.

These roles and contributions of national and international pharmacy organizations are essential for the continued growth and advancement of the pharmaceutical profession, ultimately benefiting public health on a global scale.

Pharmacy as a Career

Career Paths in Pharmacy

Pharmacy offers a diverse range of career paths, each providing unique opportunities and challenges. These paths allow pharmacists to work in various settings, contribute to different aspects of healthcare, and specialize in numerous areas of practice. Here are some of the main career paths in pharmacy:

1. Community Pharmacy

- **Description**: Community pharmacists, also known as retail pharmacists, work in local pharmacies that serve the public directly. They are the most accessible healthcare professionals for the general population.
- **Responsibilities**:

  - Dispensing prescription medications.

- Providing medication counseling and advice on the proper use of medicines.
- Managing minor ailments and recommending over-the-counter treatments.
- Conducting health screenings and providing vaccinations.
- Ensuring the safe and effective use of medication through patient education.

2. Hospital Pharmacy

- **Description**: Hospital pharmacists work within hospital settings, collaborating with other healthcare professionals to ensure the optimal use of medications in patient care.
- **Responsibilities**:

  - Preparing and dispensing medications for inpatient and outpatient use.
  - Participating in clinical rounds and advising medical staff on drug therapy.
  - Monitoring patient drug therapies and adjusting medications as needed.
  - Managing medication inventories and ensuring compliance with regulatory standards.
  - Providing specialized services such as chemotherapy preparation and parenteral nutrition.

3. Clinical Pharmacy

- **Description**: Clinical pharmacists work directly with patients and healthcare teams in various settings, including hospitals, clinics, and outpatient care centers. They focus on optimizing medication therapy and improving patient outcomes.
- **Responsibilities**:

  - Conducting comprehensive medication reviews.
  - Developing individualized medication plans.
  - Monitoring and managing chronic diseases.

- Providing drug information and education to healthcare professionals and patients.
- Participating in research and clinical trials.

4. Industrial Pharmacy

- **Description**: Industrial pharmacists work in the pharmaceutical industry, involved in the research, development, manufacturing, and quality control of medications.
- **Responsibilities**:

  - Conducting research and development of new drugs.
  - Formulating and testing drug products for safety and efficacy.
  - Ensuring compliance with regulatory standards and guidelines.
  - Overseeing the production process and quality control of pharmaceuticals.
  - Engaging in marketing, sales, and regulatory affairs.

5. Academic Pharmacy

- **Description**: Academic pharmacists work in educational institutions, such as universities and pharmacy schools, where they teach and train future pharmacists.
- **Responsibilities**:

  - Teaching courses in pharmaceutical sciences and pharmacy practice.
  - Conducting research in various fields of pharmacy and publishing findings.
  - Supervising student research projects and clinical rotations.
  - Developing and updating pharmacy curricula.
  - Engaging in community outreach and continuing education programs.

6. Regulatory Pharmacy

- **Description**: Regulatory pharmacists work with government agencies and regulatory bodies to ensure that medications and healthcare products meet safety and efficacy standards.

- **Responsibilities**:

  - Reviewing and approving new drug applications.
  - Inspecting manufacturing facilities for compliance with regulations.
  - Developing and enforcing drug policies and regulations.
  - Monitoring adverse drug reactions and ensuring post-market surveillance.
  - Providing guidance and support to pharmaceutical companies on regulatory matters.

7. Consultant Pharmacy

- **Description**: Consultant pharmacists provide expert advice on medication management to healthcare facilities, such as nursing homes, assisted living facilities, and home healthcare agencies.
- **Responsibilities**:

  - Conducting medication reviews and audits.
  - Developing and implementing medication management protocols.
  - Educating healthcare staff on best practices in medication use.
  - Monitoring and improving medication safety and efficacy.
  - Collaborating with healthcare teams to optimize patient care.

8. Research and Development

- **Description**: Pharmacists in research and development work in academic, industrial, or governmental laboratories, focusing on discovering new drugs and improving existing therapies.
- **Responsibilities**:

  - Designing and conducting experiments to identify new drug candidates.
  - Investigating the pharmacokinetics and pharmacodynamics of drugs.
  - Evaluating the safety and efficacy of new drugs through clinical trials.
  - Collaborating with multidisciplinary teams to advance drug development.
  - Publishing research findings and securing patents.

9. Pharmaceutical Marketing and Sales

- **Description**: Pharmacists in marketing and sales work for pharmaceutical companies to promote and sell their products to healthcare professionals and institutions.
- **Responsibilities**:

  - Developing marketing strategies and campaigns.
  - Educating healthcare professionals about new medications and therapies.
  - Building and maintaining relationships with healthcare providers.
  - Conducting market research to identify trends and opportunities.
  - Ensuring compliance with regulatory requirements in promotional activities.

10. Informatics Pharmacy

- **Description**: Informatics pharmacists specialize in the use of technology and data management to improve medication use and healthcare delivery.
- **Responsibilities**:

  - Implementing and maintaining electronic health records (EHR) systems.
  - Developing and optimizing clinical decision support tools.
  - Analyzing data to improve medication safety and efficacy.
  - Training healthcare staff on the use of informatics systems.
  - Collaborating with IT and clinical teams to enhance healthcare technologies.

Each of these career paths offers unique opportunities for pharmacists to utilize their expertise and contribute to different aspects of healthcare. Whether working directly with patients, conducting research, or ensuring the quality of pharmaceuticals, pharmacists play a vital role in promoting health and wellness.

Educational Requirements and Skills

A career in pharmacy requires a strong educational foundation, specialized training, and the development of various skills to ensure competence and excellence in the field. Here is an overview of the educational requirements and essential skills needed for a successful pharmacy career.

Educational Requirements

1. **Diploma in Pharmacy (D.Pharm)**

   - **Overview**: The D.Pharm program is a two-year diploma course designed to provide fundamental knowledge and skills in pharmacy. It is typically pursued after completing high school (10+2) with a focus on science subjects.
   - **Curriculum**: The curriculum includes subjects such as Pharmaceutics, Pharmaceutical Chemistry, Pharmacology, Pharmacognosy, and Hospital and Clinical Pharmacy.
   - **Career Path**: Graduates can work as pharmacy technicians or assistants in community pharmacies, hospitals, and pharmaceutical companies. They can also pursue higher studies in pharmacy.

2. **Bachelor of Pharmacy (B.Pharm)**

   - **Overview**: The B.Pharm program is a four-year undergraduate degree that provides comprehensive education in pharmaceutical sciences. It is typically pursued after completing high school (10+2) with a focus on science subjects.
   - **Curriculum**: The curriculum covers a wide range of subjects, including Human Anatomy and Physiology, Pharmaceutical Analysis, Pharmaceutics, Pharmaceutical Chemistry, Pharmacology, Pharmacognosy, and Pharmacy Practice.
   - **Career Path**: Graduates can work as pharmacists in community and hospital settings, join the pharmaceutical industry, or pursue higher education such as M.Pharm or Pharm.D.

3. **Master of Pharmacy (M.Pharm)**

   - **Overview**: The M.Pharm program is a two-year postgraduate degree that allows for specialization in various fields of pharmacy. It is typically pursued after completing a B.Pharm degree.

- **Specializations**: Specializations may include Pharmaceutical Chemistry, Pharmaceutics, Pharmacology, Pharmacognosy, Clinical Pharmacy, and Pharmaceutical Analysis.
- **Career Path**: Graduates can work in specialized roles within the pharmaceutical industry, academia, research institutions, regulatory agencies, or pursue doctoral studies (Ph.D.).

4. Doctor of Pharmacy (Pharm.D)

- **Overview**: The Pharm.D program is a six-year professional degree designed to prepare clinical pharmacists. It includes five years of academic study and one year of internship or residency.
- **Curriculum**: The curriculum covers clinical pharmacy, pharmacotherapeutics, clinical research, pharmacy practice, and patient care.
- **Career Path**: Graduates can work as clinical pharmacists in hospitals and healthcare settings, engage in clinical research, or pursue advanced clinical training.

5. Doctor of Philosophy (Ph.D.) in Pharmacy

- **Overview**: The Ph.D. program in pharmacy is a research-focused degree that involves original research and the defense of a dissertation. It is typically pursued after completing an M.Pharm degree.
- **Research Areas**: Research areas may include drug discovery, pharmaceutical technology, clinical pharmacy, pharmacokinetics, and pharmacodynamics.
- **Career Path**: Graduates can work as researchers and academicians in universities, research institutions, and the pharmaceutical industry.

Essential Skills

1. Scientific Knowledge and Technical Skills

- **Pharmacology and Therapeutics**: Understanding drug mechanisms, therapeutic uses, and adverse effects.

- **Pharmaceutical Chemistry**: Knowledge of chemical properties, synthesis, and analysis of drugs.
- **Pharmaceutics**: Skills in drug formulation, manufacturing, and quality control.
- **Clinical Pharmacy**: Expertise in patient care, medication management, and clinical decision-making.

2. Communication Skills

- **Patient Counseling**: Ability to communicate effectively with patients about medication use, side effects, and lifestyle modifications.
- **Interprofessional Collaboration**: Working effectively with other healthcare professionals to provide comprehensive patient care.
- **Public Speaking**: Presenting information clearly and confidently to groups, such as during health education sessions or professional conferences.

3. Analytical and Problem-Solving Skills

- **Critical Thinking**: Analyzing clinical data and making informed decisions regarding drug therapy.
- **Research Skills**: Conducting and interpreting research studies to advance pharmaceutical knowledge.
- **Attention to Detail**: Ensuring accuracy in prescription dispensing, compounding, and documentation.

4. Ethical and Professional Conduct

- **Integrity**: Adhering to ethical standards and professional guidelines in all aspects of practice.
- **Confidentiality**: Respecting patient privacy and maintaining the confidentiality of health information.
- **Responsibility**: Demonstrating accountability for patient outcomes and professional actions.

5. Management and Leadership Skills

- **Organizational Skills**: Efficiently managing pharmacy operations, inventory, and personnel.
- **Leadership**: Leading teams, mentoring junior pharmacists, and contributing to organizational goals.
- **Business Acumen**: Understanding the economic aspects of pharmacy practice, including cost management and financial planning.

6. **Technological Proficiency**

- **Pharmacy Informatics**: Using electronic health records (EHR), pharmacy management systems, and clinical decision support tools.
- **Data Analysis**: Interpreting clinical data and utilizing software for research and practice improvement.
- **Continuous Learning**: Keeping up-to-date with advancements in technology and integrating new tools into practice.

These educational requirements and skills are essential for pharmacists to deliver high-quality care, contribute to the healthcare team, and advance the field of pharmacy. Continuous professional development and lifelong learning are crucial for staying current with the evolving landscape of healthcare and pharmaceuticals.

Pharmacopoeias

Introduction to Pharmacopoeias

Pharmacopoeias are authoritative compendia that provide comprehensive standards for the quality, purity, strength, and consistency of medicinal substances and pharmaceutical products. These official publications serve as essential references for pharmacists, manufacturers, regulatory agencies, and healthcare providers to ensure the safety and efficacy of medicines. The role of pharmacopoeias in modern pharmacy practice cannot be overstated, as they underpin the regulatory framework governing drug production and usage.

Definition and Purpose: Pharmacopoeias are official publications that list approved drugs and medicinal substances along with their descriptions, standards of purity, chemical properties, dosage forms, and methods of analysis. The primary purpose of pharmacopoeias is to provide standardized guidelines to ensure that medicines are of high quality and safe for patient use. They serve as legal references that can be enforced by regulatory authorities to maintain the integrity of the pharmaceutical supply chain.

Historical Background: The concept of pharmacopoeias dates back to ancient civilizations where early medical practitioners documented their knowledge of medicinal plants and formulations. However, the first official pharmacopoeia, "Pharmacopoeia Augustana," was published in 1564 in Augsburg, Germany. Since then, many countries have developed their own pharmacopoeias to cater to their specific healthcare needs.

Functions of Pharmacopoeias:

1. **Standardization:**

   - Pharmacopoeias establish standardized methods for drug preparation and testing, ensuring consistency across different batches of medicines. This standardization is crucial for maintaining drug quality and effectiveness.

2. **Quality Assurance:**

   - By defining quality parameters and acceptable limits for impurities, pharmacopoeias help prevent the distribution of substandard or counterfeit medications. They provide detailed protocols for the identification, assay, and purity testing of drugs.

3. **Regulatory Compliance:**

   - Pharmacopoeias serve as legal documents that are recognized by regulatory authorities. Compliance with pharmacopoeial standards is mandatory for the approval and marketing of pharmaceutical products. This ensures that manufacturers adhere to strict quality controls.

4. **Reference for Formulations:**

   - Pharmacopoeias provide detailed formulations and preparation methods for various dosage forms, including tablets, capsules, injections, and topical applications. This serves as a valuable reference for pharmacists and pharmaceutical scientists involved in drug formulation and compounding.

5. **Guidance for New Drug Development**:

- Pharmacopoeias offer guidelines on the development and testing of new drugs. They outline the required specifications and testing methods that new drugs must meet to ensure they are safe and effective for patient use.

Major Pharmacopoeias:

1. **Indian Pharmacopoeia (IP)**:

- The Indian Pharmacopoeia is the official pharmacopoeia of India, published by the Indian Pharmacopoeia Commission (IPC). It sets standards for drugs and pharmaceutical products used in India and is recognized by the Ministry of Health and Family Welfare.

2. **British Pharmacopoeia (BP)**:

- The British Pharmacopoeia is the official pharmacopoeia of the United Kingdom, published by the British Pharmacopoeia Commission. It provides standards for medicines and is widely used in many countries around the world.

3. **United States Pharmacopeia (USP)**:

- The United States Pharmacopeia is a compendium of drug standards published by the United States Pharmacopeial Convention. It sets quality standards for drugs, dietary supplements, and food ingredients in the United States and is recognized globally.

4. **European Pharmacopoeia (Ph. Eur.)**:

- The European Pharmacopoeia is a harmonized pharmacopoeia for Europe, published by the European Directorate for the Quality of Medicines & HealthCare (EDQM). It sets common standards for medicinal products across Europe to ensure their quality and safety.

5. **International Pharmacopoeia (Int. Ph.):**

- Published by the World Health Organization (WHO), the International Pharmacopoeia provides global standards for pharmaceutical substances and dosage forms. It is particularly useful for countries that do not have their own national pharmacopoeia.

Evolution and Updates: Pharmacopoeias are dynamic documents that evolve with advancements in pharmaceutical science and technology. Regular updates are essential to incorporate new research findings, emerging drug therapies, and improved analytical methods. Pharmacopoeial commissions and committees continuously review and revise the content to reflect current best practices and scientific knowledge.

Pharmacopoeias play a critical role in the healthcare system by ensuring the quality, safety, and efficacy of medicinal products. They provide the foundational standards that guide the pharmaceutical industry, regulatory authorities, and healthcare professionals in delivering high-quality healthcare. Understanding and adhering to pharmacopoeial standards is fundamental for anyone involved in the development, manufacture, regulation, and dispensing of medications.

IP (Indian Pharmacopoeia)

The **Indian Pharmacopoeia (IP)** is the official pharmacopoeia of India, serving as a critical reference for standards of drug quality, purity, and strength in the country. Published by the **Indian Pharmacopoeia Commission (IPC)**, the IP is recognized by the **Ministry of Health and Family Welfare** and is an essential tool for pharmaceutical manufacturers, healthcare professionals, and regulatory authorities.

Historical Background: The Indian Pharmacopoeia has a rich history dating back to its first edition in 1955. The need for a national pharmacopoeia was recognized to ensure the availability of quality medicines in the country. Prior to the IP, India primarily relied on the British Pharmacopoeia (BP) and other international standards. The first edition was prepared under the guidance of the Indian Pharmacopoeia Committee, and subsequent editions have been periodically updated to include advancements in pharmaceutical sciences and emerging healthcare needs.

Objectives and Purpose: The primary objective of the IP is to provide standards for the identity, purity, and strength of drugs and pharmaceutical products. These standards ensure that medicines available in India meet the required quality specifications, thereby protecting public health. The IP serves several purposes:

- **Standardization**: Establishing consistent methods and criteria for drug quality assessment.
- **Regulation**: Providing a legal and scientific basis for the regulation and control of pharmaceutical products.
- **Quality Assurance**: Ensuring the safety and efficacy of medicines through rigorous testing and validation protocols.

Structure and Content: The Indian Pharmacopoeia is divided into several volumes and sections, each addressing different aspects of pharmaceutical standards. Key components include:

- **Monographs**: Detailed descriptions of individual drugs and pharmaceutical substances, including their physical and chemical properties, identification tests, purity criteria, and assay methods.
- **General Chapters**: Comprehensive guidelines on analytical techniques, standard operating procedures, and laboratory practices. This section includes methodologies for drug testing, equipment calibration, and validation of analytical methods.
- **Appendices**: Supplementary information and reference tables, such as molecular weights, conversion factors, and lists of reagents and solutions used in pharmacopoeial tests.

Monographs: Monographs form the core of the Indian Pharmacopoeia. Each monograph provides detailed specifications for an individual drug or pharmaceutical product, including:

- **Description**: Physical appearance, solubility, and other relevant characteristics.
- **Identification Tests**: Methods to confirm the identity of the substance, ensuring it matches the specified drug.

- **Purity Tests**: Criteria for detecting impurities and contaminants, ensuring the drug meets purity standards.
- **Assay Methods**: Quantitative procedures to determine the drug's potency and concentration.

General Chapters: General chapters cover a wide range of topics related to pharmaceutical analysis and quality control, including:

- **Analytical Techniques**: Methods such as chromatography, spectrophotometry, and titration used for drug testing and analysis.
- **Microbiological Standards**: Guidelines for sterility testing, microbial limit tests, and antimicrobial efficacy.
- **Packaging and Storage**: Requirements for the packaging, labeling, and storage of pharmaceutical products to maintain their stability and integrity.

Appendices: Appendices provide additional reference information and support the implementation of standards outlined in the monographs and general chapters. They include:

- **Reference Standards**: Lists of official standards and reference materials used for calibration and validation.
- **Reagents and Solutions**: Specifications for the preparation and standardization of chemical reagents and solutions used in analytical procedures.
- **Supplementary Tables**: Tables for molecular weights, temperature conversions, and other useful data for laboratory work.

Revision and Updates: The Indian Pharmacopoeia is periodically revised to incorporate new scientific knowledge, advancements in pharmaceutical technology, and emerging public health needs. The **Indian Pharmacopoeia Commission (IPC)**, established in 2009, is responsible for overseeing the preparation and publication of the IP. The IPC collaborates with various stakeholders, including pharmaceutical industries, academic institutions, research organizations, and regulatory authorities, to ensure the pharmacopoeia remains current and relevant.

Significance and Impact: The Indian Pharmacopoeia plays a crucial role in the Indian healthcare system by:

- **Ensuring Drug Quality**: Establishing and maintaining high standards for pharmaceutical products to protect public health.
- **Supporting Regulatory Framework**: Providing a legal basis for the regulation of drugs and enforcement of quality standards by regulatory agencies such as the Central Drugs Standard Control Organization (CDSCO).
- **Facilitating International Trade**: Harmonizing with international pharmacopoeial standards, thereby facilitating the export of Indian pharmaceutical products to global markets.
- **Promoting Public Health**: Ensuring the availability of safe, effective, and affordable medicines for the Indian population.

In conclusion, the Indian Pharmacopoeia is an indispensable resource that upholds the standards of pharmaceutical quality in India. It ensures that medicines meet rigorous quality criteria, thereby safeguarding public health and supporting the country's pharmaceutical industry in producing world-class products.

BP (British Pharmacopoeia)

The **British Pharmacopoeia (BP)** is one of the most respected and widely used pharmacopoeias globally. It provides authoritative standards for the quality of medicines and their constituents, ensuring their safety and efficacy. The BP is published by the British Pharmacopoeia Commission under the authority of the United Kingdom's Medicines and Healthcare products Regulatory Agency (MHRA).

Historical Background: The British Pharmacopoeia has a rich history, with its first edition published in 1864. It was created to unify the various regional pharmacopoeias in the United Kingdom into a single, authoritative reference. Over the years, the BP has undergone numerous revisions and updates to reflect advances in pharmaceutical science and changes in medical practice. The BP is updated annually to ensure it remains current and relevant.

Objectives and Purpose: The primary objective of the BP is to establish comprehensive and authoritative standards for the quality, purity, and strength of medicines and their ingredients. These standards are essential for ensuring the safety and efficacy of pharmaceutical products used in the United Kingdom and many other countries.

Structure and Content: The British Pharmacopoeia is organized into several volumes, each addressing different aspects of pharmaceutical standards. The key components include:

- **Monographs**: Detailed descriptions of individual drugs, including their physical and chemical properties, identification tests, purity criteria, and assay methods.
- **General Notices**: Guidelines and principles that apply to the entire pharmacopoeia, including definitions, general requirements, and standards for pharmaceutical practices.
- **General Chapters**: Detailed information on analytical techniques, equipment calibration, and standard operating procedures used in drug testing and quality control.
- **Appendices**: Supplementary information, including reference tables, lists of reagents, and standard solutions used in pharmacopoeial tests.

Monographs: Monographs are the core of the British Pharmacopoeia, providing specific details for each drug or pharmaceutical substance. Each monograph includes:

- **Description**: Physical appearance, solubility, and other relevant characteristics.
- **Identification Tests**: Methods to confirm the identity of the substance, ensuring it matches the specified drug.
- **Purity Tests**: Criteria for detecting impurities and contaminants, ensuring the drug meets purity standards.
- **Assay Methods**: Quantitative procedures to determine the drug's potency and concentration.

General Notices: General notices provide overarching guidelines that apply to all sections of the BP. They include definitions of terms used throughout the pharmacopoeia, principles for interpreting monographs, and standards for pharmaceutical practices. General notices ensure consistency and clarity in the application of BP standards.

General Chapters: General chapters cover a wide range of topics related to pharmaceutical analysis and quality control. These chapters provide detailed methodologies for analytical techniques such as chromatography, spectrophotometry, and titration. They also include guidelines for equipment calibration, method validation, and microbiological testing.

Appendices: Appendices provide additional reference information to support the implementation of standards outlined in the monographs and general chapters. They include lists of official reference standards, reagents, and solutions, as well as tables for molecular weights, temperature conversions, and other useful data for laboratory work.

Revision and Updates: The British Pharmacopoeia is revised and updated annually to incorporate new scientific knowledge, advancements in pharmaceutical technology, and changes in regulatory requirements. The British Pharmacopoeia Commission oversees the preparation and publication of the BP, ensuring it remains a relevant and authoritative resource. The Commission collaborates with experts from academia, industry, and regulatory bodies to review and update the content.

Significance and Impact: The British Pharmacopoeia plays a crucial role in the global pharmaceutical landscape by:

- **Ensuring Drug Quality**: Establishing and maintaining high standards for pharmaceutical products to ensure their safety, efficacy, and quality.
- **Supporting Regulatory Framework**: Providing a legal basis for the regulation of medicines and enforcement of quality standards by regulatory authorities such as the MHRA.
- **Facilitating International Trade**: Harmonizing with other international pharmacopoeial standards, thereby facilitating the export and import of pharmaceutical products.
- **Promoting Public Health**: Ensuring that medicines available to the public meet rigorous quality criteria, thereby protecting public health.

International Influence: The British Pharmacopoeia is not only a key reference in the United Kingdom but also holds significant influence internationally. Many countries use the BP as a reference for their own national pharmacopoeias or adopt its standards directly. This widespread use underscores the BP's role in promoting global harmonization of pharmaceutical standards and practices.

The British Pharmacopoeia is an indispensable resource in the field of pharmaceutical sciences. Its comprehensive standards for drug quality, safety, and efficacy ensure that medicines are of the highest quality. The BP's continuous evolution and adherence to scientific advancements make it a critical tool for regulatory authorities, pharmaceutical manufacturers, healthcare professionals, and researchers worldwide. Understanding and adhering to the standards set by the BP is essential for anyone involved in the development, manufacture, regulation, and dispensing of pharmaceutical products.

Pharmacopoeias

USP (United States Pharmacopeia)

The **United States Pharmacopeia (USP)** is a highly respected and widely used compendium of drug standards, established to ensure the quality, purity, strength, and consistency of medicines. The USP sets legally enforceable standards recognized by the United States Food and Drug Administration (FDA) and is used as a reference globally.

Historical Background: The USP was first published in 1820, making it one of the oldest continuously published pharmacopeias. It was created by a group of eleven physicians in Washington, D.C., who aimed to standardize drug formulations in the United States. The USP has undergone numerous updates and revisions since its inception, reflecting advances in medical science and changes in pharmaceutical practices.

Objectives and Purpose: The primary objective of the USP is to establish publicly available standards for medicines, food ingredients, and dietary supplements. These standards ensure that products are of high quality, safe, and effective for consumer use. The USP serves several key purposes:

- **Standardization**: Providing consistent methods and criteria for drug quality assessment.
- **Regulation**: Offering a legal framework for the regulation and control of pharmaceutical products.
- **Quality Assurance**: Ensuring the safety and efficacy of medicines through rigorous testing and validation protocols.

Structure and Content: The United States Pharmacopeia is published in conjunction with the National Formulary (NF), and together they are referred to as USP-NF. The USP-NF is organized into several volumes, each addressing different aspects of pharmaceutical standards. The key components include:

- **Monographs**: Detailed descriptions of individual drugs and pharmaceutical substances, including their physical and chemical properties, identification tests, purity criteria, and assay methods.
- **General Chapters**: Comprehensive guidelines on analytical techniques, standard operating procedures, and laboratory practices. This section includes methodologies for drug testing, equipment calibration, and validation of analytical methods.
- **General Notices**: Guidelines and principles that apply to the entire USP-NF, including definitions, general requirements, and standards for pharmaceutical practices.
- **Supplements**: Periodic updates to the USP-NF that include new and revised monographs and general chapters.

Monographs: Monographs form the core of the USP, providing specific details for each drug or pharmaceutical substance. Each monograph includes:

- **Description**: Physical appearance, solubility, and other relevant characteristics.
- **Identification Tests**: Methods to confirm the identity of the substance, ensuring it matches the specified drug.
- **Purity Tests**: Criteria for detecting impurities and contaminants, ensuring the drug meets purity standards.
- **Assay Methods**: Quantitative procedures to determine the drug's potency and concentration.

General Chapters: General chapters cover a wide range of topics related to pharmaceutical analysis and quality control. These chapters provide detailed methodologies for analytical techniques such as chromatography, spectrophotometry, and titration. They also include guidelines for equipment calibration, method validation, microbiological testing, and compounding practices.

General Notices: General notices provide overarching guidelines that apply to all sections of the USP-NF. They include definitions of terms used throughout the pharmacopoeia, principles for interpreting monographs, and standards for pharmaceutical practices. General notices ensure consistency and clarity in the application of USP-NF standards.

Supplements: Supplements are issued periodically to update the USP-NF with new and revised monographs and general chapters. These updates ensure that the compendium remains current with scientific advancements and regulatory requirements.

Revision and Updates: The United States Pharmacopeia is regularly revised and updated to incorporate new scientific knowledge, advancements in pharmaceutical technology, and changes in regulatory requirements. The USP Convention, a nonprofit organization, oversees the preparation and publication of the USP-NF. The Convention collaborates with experts from academia, industry, and regulatory bodies to review and update the content.

Significance and Impact: The USP plays a crucial role in the global pharmaceutical landscape by:

- **Ensuring Drug Quality**: Establishing and maintaining high standards for pharmaceutical products to ensure their safety, efficacy, and quality.
- **Supporting Regulatory Framework**: Providing a legal basis for the regulation of medicines and enforcement of quality standards by regulatory authorities such as the FDA.
- **Facilitating International Trade**: Harmonizing with other international pharmacopoeial standards, thereby facilitating the export and import of pharmaceutical products.
- **Promoting Public Health**: Ensuring that medicines available to the public meet rigorous quality criteria, thereby protecting public health.

International Influence: The USP is not only a key reference in the United States but also holds significant influence internationally. Many countries use the USP as a reference for their own national pharmacopoeias or adopt its standards directly. This widespread use underscores the USP's role in promoting global harmonization of pharmaceutical standards and practices.

The United States Pharmacopeia is an indispensable resource in the field of pharmaceutical sciences. Its comprehensive standards for drug quality, safety, and efficacy ensure that medicines are of the highest quality. The USP's continuous evolution and adherence to scientific advancements make it a critical tool for regulatory authorities, pharmaceutical manufacturers, healthcare professionals, and researchers worldwide. Understanding and adhering to the standards set by the USP is essential for anyone involved in the development, manufacture, regulation, and dispensing of pharmaceutical products.

Extra Pharmacopoeia

The **Extra Pharmacopoeia**, also known as **Martindale: The Complete Drug Reference**, is a comprehensive and authoritative reference work used by healthcare professionals worldwide. Unlike official pharmacopoeias, which are legal standards published by governmental or regulatory bodies, the Extra Pharmacopoeia serves as an extensive guide to drugs and medicinal products, providing detailed information on their uses, dosages, pharmacokinetics, and pharmacodynamics.

Historical Background: The Extra Pharmacopoeia was first published in 1883 by William Martindale, a pharmacist and medical writer, and has since become a vital resource for pharmacists, physicians, and other healthcare professionals. Over the years, it has undergone numerous revisions and updates to include the latest information on drug therapy and pharmaceutical science.

Objectives and Purpose: The primary objective of the Extra Pharmacopoeia is to provide comprehensive and reliable information on a wide range of drugs and medicinal substances. Its purpose is to serve as a reference for healthcare professionals in clinical practice, enabling them to make informed decisions about drug therapy and patient care.

Structure and Content: The Extra Pharmacopoeia is organized into several sections, each providing detailed information on various aspects of drugs and medicinal products. The key components include:

- **Monographs**: Detailed entries for individual drugs, including their pharmacological properties, therapeutic uses, side effects, interactions, and dosage forms.
- **Clinical Information**: Comprehensive guidelines on the clinical use of drugs, including indications, contraindications, precautions, and monitoring requirements.
- **Pharmaceutical Information**: Data on the chemical properties, stability, storage, and preparation of drugs.
- **Therapeutic Index**: An index of therapeutic uses and conditions, providing a quick reference for healthcare professionals.

- **Appendices**: Supplementary information, including drug interactions, adverse reactions, and guidelines for special populations such as pediatric and geriatric patients.

Monographs: Monographs are the core of the Extra Pharmacopoeia, offering in-depth information on individual drugs. Each monograph includes:

- **Description**: Physical and chemical properties of the drug.
- **Pharmacology**: Mechanism of action, pharmacokinetics, and pharmacodynamics.
- **Therapeutic Uses**: Indications and clinical applications.
- **Dosage and Administration**: Recommended dosages for different conditions and patient populations.
- **Side Effects and Adverse Reactions**: Potential side effects and management of adverse reactions.
- **Drug Interactions**: Information on interactions with other drugs, food, and medical conditions.
- **Contraindications and Precautions**: Situations where the drug should not be used and necessary precautions.

Clinical Information: This section provides practical guidelines for the clinical use of drugs, helping healthcare professionals to:

- **Identify appropriate treatments** for various medical conditions.
- **Understand contraindications and precautions** to avoid adverse effects.
- **Monitor patient response** to therapy and adjust treatment plans accordingly.

Pharmaceutical Information: The pharmaceutical information section includes:

- **Chemical Properties**: Details about the chemical structure and properties of drugs.
- **Stability and Storage**: Guidelines for the proper storage of drugs to maintain their efficacy and safety.
- **Preparation and Compounding**: Instructions for preparing and compounding drugs, especially for formulations not commercially

available.

Therapeutic Index: The therapeutic index provides a comprehensive list of therapeutic uses and conditions, allowing healthcare professionals to:

- **Quickly find appropriate drug therapies** for specific medical conditions.
- **Cross-reference indications** with other sections of the Extra Pharmacopoeia for detailed information.

Appendices: The appendices offer additional resources and information, including:

- **Drug Interactions**: Detailed tables and descriptions of potential interactions between drugs.
- **Adverse Reactions**: Comprehensive lists of known adverse reactions and their management.
- **Special Populations**: Guidelines for dosing and monitoring in special populations such as children, elderly patients, and pregnant or breastfeeding women.

Revision and Updates: The Extra Pharmacopoeia is regularly updated to incorporate new drugs, emerging therapies, and the latest research findings. These updates ensure that the information remains current and relevant for clinical practice. The editorial team collaborates with experts from various fields to review and revise the content.

Significance and Impact: The Extra Pharmacopoeia plays a crucial role in the global healthcare landscape by:

- **Providing Reliable Information**: Offering comprehensive and accurate data on drugs and their use, supporting evidence-based practice.
- **Enhancing Clinical Decision-Making**: Equipping healthcare professionals with the knowledge needed to make informed decisions about drug therapy.
- **Improving Patient Care**: Contributing to the safe and effective use of medicines, thereby improving patient outcomes.
- **Supporting Continuing Education**: Serving as a valuable resource for the ongoing education and professional development of healthcare

providers.

International Influence: The Extra Pharmacopoeia is recognized and used by healthcare professionals around the world. Its comprehensive coverage and authoritative content make it a valuable reference in various clinical settings, including hospitals, clinics, pharmacies, and research institutions.

The Extra Pharmacopoeia, or Martindale: The Complete Drug Reference, is an indispensable resource in the field of pharmacy and medicine. Its extensive and detailed information on drugs and medicinal products ensures that healthcare professionals have access to the knowledge necessary for high-quality patient care. Understanding and utilizing the information provided by the Extra Pharmacopoeia is essential for anyone involved in the prescribing, dispensing, and administration of medications

CHAPTER TWO

Introduction to Dosage Forms

Definition

A dosage form is a specific formulation or physical form in which a drug is produced and administered to patients. Dosage forms include solids, liquids, semi-solids, and gases, each tailored to meet specific therapeutic needs and patient preferences. The term encompasses a wide range of preparations such as tablets, capsules, injections, syrups, ointments, and aerosols, among others. Dosage forms play a crucial role in the therapeutic process by ensuring that drugs are delivered to the body in a controlled and effective manner.

Importance

The importance of dosage forms lies in their ability to optimize drug delivery. Different dosage forms are designed to achieve various objectives, such as:

- **Enhancing Drug Stability**: Protecting the active ingredients from degradation due to environmental factors like light, moisture, and air.
- **Controlling Release Rates**: Modifying the release of the drug to provide sustained or delayed therapeutic effects.
- **Improving Bioavailability**: Enhancing the fraction of the administered dose that reaches the systemic circulation.
- **Ensuring Patient Compliance**: Providing convenient, easy-to-use formulations that encourage patients to adhere to their medication regimens.
- **Targeting Drug Delivery**: Delivering drugs directly to the site of action to improve efficacy and reduce side effects.

For instance, oral tablets and capsules are popular for their convenience and accurate dosing, making them ideal for self-administration. Liquid forms like syrups and solutions are often preferred for pediatric and geriatric patients who may have difficulty swallowing solids. Specialized forms such as transdermal patches and inhalers offer unique advantages by providing continuous drug delivery and targeting specific sites within the body.

Historical Context

The concept of dosage forms dates back to ancient times when early humans used natural substances for medicinal purposes. Ancient civilizations like the Egyptians, Greeks, and Chinese developed various forms of administering medications, such as herbal concoctions, poultices, and ointments. These rudimentary dosage forms were primarily derived from plants and minerals and were used to treat various ailments.

The evolution of dosage forms progressed significantly with the advent of modern chemistry and pharmacology in the 19th and 20th centuries. The development of synthetic drugs and the understanding of pharmacokinetics and pharmacodynamics led to the creation of more sophisticated dosage forms. Innovations such as controlled-release tablets, injectable formulations, and inhalation devices have greatly expanded the range of therapeutic options available.

The Need for Dosage Forms

Dosage forms are needed for several reasons:

1. **Protection of Drug Substances**: Many active pharmaceutical ingredients (APIs) are sensitive to environmental factors such as light, moisture, and temperature. Dosage forms can protect these substances from degradation and extend their shelf life.
2. **Accurate Dosage**: Dosage forms provide a precise amount of the drug in each unit, ensuring accurate dosing and reducing the risk of under- or overdosing.
3. **Convenient Administration**: Different dosage forms cater to different patient needs and preferences, making it easier for patients to take their medications as prescribed. For example, liquid forms are easier for

children and elderly patients, while transdermal patches offer a non-invasive alternative for those who cannot take oral medications.

4. **Controlled Release**: Dosage forms can be designed to release the drug at a specific rate, providing sustained therapeutic effects and reducing the frequency of dosing.

5. **Targeted Delivery**: Some dosage forms are engineered to deliver the drug directly to the site of action, enhancing therapeutic efficacy and minimizing systemic side effects.

6. **Enhanced Patient Compliance**: Convenient and palatable dosage forms improve patient adherence to treatment regimens, which is crucial for the effectiveness of the therapy.

Development of Dosage Forms

The development of dosage forms involves meticulous planning and consideration of various factors, including:

- **Physicochemical Properties of the Drug**: The solubility, stability, and compatibility of the drug with excipients (inactive ingredients) are critical considerations.
- **Route of Administration**: The intended route of administration (oral, topical, intravenous, etc.) influences the choice of dosage form.
- **Patient Population**: Age, health condition, and preferences of the target patient population are taken into account to ensure the dosage form is suitable and acceptable.
- **Therapeutic Goals**: The desired therapeutic outcomes, such as rapid onset of action or prolonged effect, guide the design of the dosage form.

Dosage forms are integral to the practice of pharmacy and medicine. They play a pivotal role in the effective and safe delivery of medications by facilitating correct administration, optimizing absorption, and enhancing patient adherence to treatment regimens. The evolution and development of dosage forms have been driven by the need to improve drug efficacy, stability, and patient convenience, making them a cornerstone of modern therapeutics.

Types and Classifications

Dosage forms can be broadly classified into several types based on their physical state, route of administration, and intended use. Each classification serves a unique purpose and is designed to meet specific therapeutic needs and patient preferences. The main categories include solid, liquid, semi-solid, and gaseous dosage forms.

Solid Dosage Forms

Solid dosage forms are among the most common and include tablets, capsules, powders, granules, lozenges, and more.

- **Tablets**: Tablets are solid units of medication that come in various shapes, sizes, and types. They can be uncoated or coated (such as enteric-coated or film-coated) to improve taste, protect the drug from environmental factors, or control the release rate. There are different types of tablets such as chewable tablets, effervescent tablets, sublingual tablets, buccal tablets, and orally disintegrating tablets (ODTs). Each type is designed for specific routes of administration or therapeutic effects. For example, sublingual tablets dissolve under the tongue for rapid absorption, while enteric-coated tablets protect the drug from stomach acid and release it in the intestines.

- **Capsules**: Capsules consist of drugs enclosed within a gelatin shell, which can be either hard or soft. Hard gelatin capsules typically contain powdered or pelletized drug forms, while soft gelatin capsules are used for oils and active ingredients that are dissolved or suspended in oil. Capsules offer an advantage in masking unpleasant tastes and odors, and they can provide a quicker onset of action compared to tablets. Modified-release capsules can provide extended or controlled drug release.

- **Powders**: Powders are finely divided drug particles that can be used internally or externally. Internal powders can be taken orally, inhaled, or dissolved in a liquid before administration. External powders are applied to the skin for their drying and soothing effects. Powders offer flexible dosing and rapid absorption, especially when dissolved in a liquid. They are often used in reconstitution for oral or injectable solutions.

- **Granules**: Granules are agglomerates of powder particles used to improve flow properties and stability. They are often used in the preparation of tablets and capsules, or as sachets for oral administration. Granules dissolve or disperse quickly when added to a liquid, making them suitable for pediatric or geriatric patients who may have difficulty swallowing tablets or capsules.

- **Lozenges and Troches**: Lozenges and troches are solid dosage forms intended to dissolve slowly in the mouth. They are commonly used for delivering medications locally to the mouth and throat, such as anesthetics, antiseptics, or cough suppressants.

Tablets	Solid units, various shapes and sizes, often coated	Accurate dosing, convenient for self-administration, stable	Chewable tablets, effervescent tablets, enteric-coated tablets
Capsules	Drug enclosed within a gelatin shell, can be hard or soft	Masks unpleasant tastes/odors, quick onset of action	Hard gelatin capsules, soft gelatin capsules
Powders	Finely divided drug particles, used internally or externally	Flexible dosing, rapid absorption	Oral powders, inhalation powders
Granules	Agglomerates of powder particles	Improved flow properties and stability	Sachets, effervescent granules
Lozenges	Solid, dissolves slowly in the mouth	Local treatment for mouth/throat conditions	Throat lozenges, cough drops

Solid dosage forms

Liquid Dosage Forms

Liquid dosage forms include solutions, suspensions, emulsions, elixirs, syrups, and tinctures.

- **Solutions**: Solutions are clear liquids where the drug is completely dissolved in a solvent, making them easy to absorb. They are used for oral, injectable, and topical administration. Oral solutions are convenient for pediatric and geriatric patients, while injectable solutions provide rapid drug action. Topical solutions are used for local effects on the skin or mucous membranes.
- **Suspensions**: Suspensions contain finely divided drug particles suspended in a liquid medium. They require shaking before use to ensure uniform dosing. Suspensions are ideal for drugs that are not soluble in

water and are commonly used in oral, topical, and injectable forms. Oral suspensions are often flavored to improve palatability.

- **Emulsions**: Emulsions are mixtures of two immiscible liquids, one of which is dispersed as small droplets within the other, stabilized by emulsifying agents. They are used for oral, topical, and parenteral administration. Emulsions provide a means to deliver lipophilic drugs in an aqueous medium, improving bioavailability and patient acceptance.
- **Elixirs**: Elixirs are clear, sweetened, hydroalcoholic solutions intended for oral use. They are used to dissolve drugs that are not soluble in water alone. Elixirs provide a pleasant taste and can contain flavoring agents to improve palatability.
- **Syrups**: Syrups are concentrated aqueous solutions of sugar or sugar substitutes, often used to mask the taste of unpleasant drugs. They are used for oral administration, especially in pediatric patients. Syrups can be medicated (containing active drug ingredients) or non-medicated (used as vehicles for drug administration).
- **Tinctures**: Tinctures are alcoholic or hydroalcoholic solutions prepared from vegetable materials or chemical substances. They are used for oral or topical administration. Tinctures are highly concentrated and require careful dosing.

Solutions	Drug completely dissolved in a solvent	Easy absorption, various routes of administration	Oral solutions, injectable solutions
Suspensions	Finely divided drug particles suspended in liquid	Ideal for insoluble drugs, requires shaking	Oral suspensions, topical suspensions
Emulsions	Mixtures of two immiscible liquids	Improves bioavailability of lipophilic drugs	Oral emulsions, topical emulsions
Elixirs	Clear, sweetened, hydroalcoholic solutions	Pleasant taste, good solubility for certain drugs	Cough elixirs, antihistamine elixirs
Syrups	Concentrated aqueous solutions of sugar	Masks unpleasant tastes, suitable for pediatric use	Cough syrups, vitamin syrups
Tinctures	Alcoholic or hydroalcoholic solutions	Highly concentrated, good for certain plant extracts	Iodine tincture, herbal tinctures

Liqiuid dosage form

Semi-Solid Dosage Forms

Semi-solid dosage forms include ointments, creams, gels, pastes, and poultices.

- **Ointments**: Ointments are greasy preparations used for their emollient effect and are often applied to the skin. They provide a protective barrier and are used for their moisturizing and therapeutic properties. Ointments are suitable for delivering drugs to the skin or mucous membranes.
- **Creams**: Creams are emulsions with a higher water content than ointments, making them less greasy and easier to spread. They are used for both medicinal and cosmetic purposes, providing hydration and delivering active ingredients to the skin. Creams can be oil-in-water (O/W) or water-in-oil (W/O) emulsions.
- **Gels**: Gels are jelly-like substances that provide a cooling effect and are easily absorbed by the skin. They are used for topical drug delivery and can be formulated to deliver drugs transdermally or through mucosal membranes. Gels can be aqueous or alcoholic and may contain various gelling agents to provide the desired consistency.
- **Pastes**: Pastes are thick preparations that adhere well to the skin, used for their protective and therapeutic effects. They are often used in conditions requiring prolonged contact with the skin, such as diaper rash or psoriasis. Pastes contain a higher proportion of solid material compared to ointments, making them more stiff and less greasy.
- **Poultices**: Poultices are soft, moist masses of material applied to the body to relieve soreness and inflammation. They are typically made from plant materials and applied warm to the skin. Poultices can provide local heat and moisture, promoting circulation and relaxation.

Dosage Form	Characteristics	Advantages	Examples
Ointments	Greasy preparations, used topically	Provides a protective barrier, moisturizing	Antibacterial ointments, emollient ointments
Creams	Emulsions with higher water content	Less greasy, easier to spread	Hydrocortisone cream, moisturizing cream
Gels	Jelly-like substances	Cooling effect, easily absorbed	Topical anesthetic gels, anti-inflammatory gels
Pastes	Thick preparations, adheres well to the skin	Protective and therapeutic effects	Zinc oxide paste, dental pastes
Poultices	Soft, moist masses applied to the body	Relieves soreness and inflammation	Herbal poultices, clay poultices

Semi-solid dosage forms

Gaseous Dosage Forms

-

Aerosols, inhalers, and sprays.

- **Aerosols:** Aerosols are pressurized dosage forms that deliver the drug in the form of a fine mist or spray, commonly used for respiratory conditions. They provide a convenient and efficient means of delivering medication directly to the lungs. Aerosols can be metered-dose inhalers (MDIs) or nebulizers, which convert liquid medication into a fine mist for inhalation.

- **Inhalers**: Inhalers are devices that deliver a specific dose of medication to the lungs, providing rapid relief from conditions like asthma and COPD. They can be metered-dose inhalers (MDIs), dry powder inhalers (DPIs), or soft mist inhalers (SMIs), each offering unique advantages in drug delivery and patient use.
- **Sprays**: Sprays are solutions or suspensions that are delivered as a fine mist or droplets through a spray nozzle. They are used for local or systemic administration, such as nasal sprays for allergic rhinitis or topical sprays for wound care.

Dosage Form	Characteristics	Advantages	Examples
Aerosols	Pressurized, delivers drug as a fine mist	Efficient for respiratory conditions	Asthma inhalers, nasal sprays
Inhalers	Devices delivering specific doses to lungs	Rapid relief, targeted delivery	Metered-dose inhalers (MDIs), dry powder inhalers (DPIs)
Sprays	Solutions/suspensions delivered as a fine mist	Local or systemic administration	Nasal sprays, topical sprays

Gaseous dosage forms

Specialized Dosage Forms

Beyond the basic types, there are specialized dosage forms designed for specific delivery methods.

- **Transdermal Patches**: Transdermal patches deliver drugs through the skin into the bloodstream over an extended period. They provide a controlled release of medication, improving patient compliance and maintaining steady drug levels. Transdermal patches are used for a variety of conditions, including pain management, hormone replacement therapy, and smoking cessation.
- **Suppositories**: Suppositories are solid forms meant to dissolve or melt in body cavities like the rectum or vagina, offering an alternative route for systemic or local action. They are useful for patients who cannot

take drugs orally or need localized treatment. Suppositories provide a convenient method for delivering medications that can bypass the gastrointestinal tract.

- **Parenteral Preparations**: Parenteral preparations include injectable forms that are administered directly into the bloodstream, muscles, or tissues. They provide rapid and controlled drug delivery, essential for emergency situations or when oral administration is not feasible. Parenteral preparations can be solutions, suspensions, or emulsions, and they require sterile conditions for administration.
- **Buccal and Sublingual Tablets**: Buccal and sublingual tablets are designed to dissolve in the mouth, allowing for rapid absorption through the mucous membranes. Buccal tablets are placed between the gum and cheek, while sublingual tablets are placed under the tongue. These routes provide a quick onset of action and bypass the first-pass metabolism in the liver.
- **Implants**: Implants are long-acting dosage forms that are surgically placed under the skin or within the body. They provide continuous drug release over extended periods, ranging from months to years. Implants are used for various medical conditions, including contraception, hormone therapy, and chronic pain management.

The choice of dosage form is crucial and depends on various factors, including the drug's physicochemical properties, the disease being treated, the patient's condition, and the route of administration. Each form is tailored to optimize the therapeutic effect, ensure patient compliance, and improve the overall efficacy of the treatment. The development of dosage forms involves meticulous planning and consideration of these factors to ensure that the final product is safe, effective, and acceptable to patients.

Dosage Form	Characteristics	Advantages	Examples
Transdermal Patches	Delivers drugs through skin over extended periods	Controlled release, improved compliance	Nicotine patches, hormone replacement patches
Suppositories	Solid, dissolves/melts in body cavities	Alternative for patients who can't take oral drugs	Rectal suppositories, vaginal suppositories
Parenteral Preparations	Injectable forms, administered directly	Rapid, controlled delivery	Intravenous solutions, intramuscular injections
Buccal/Sublingual Tablets	Dissolves in the mouth, rapid absorption	Bypasses first-pass metabolism	Buccal tablets, sublingual nitroglycerin
Implants	Surgically placed, long-acting	Continuous drug release	Contraceptive implants, hormone implants

Specialized Dosage Forms

CHAPTER THREE

Prescription

Definition of a Prescription

A prescription is a formal written order by a licensed healthcare professional, such as a doctor or nurse practitioner, authorizing a patient to be provided with a specific medicine or treatment. This legal document ensures the correct administration of medications by detailing the drug name, dosage, and instructions for use. Prescriptions play a critical role in the healthcare system by ensuring medications are used safely and effectively.

Historical Context of Prescriptions

Prescriptions have a long history, dating back to ancient civilizations where healers and physicians recommended treatments. Over centuries, the format and use of prescriptions have evolved, becoming more standardized and regulated to ensure patient safety and proper drug administration. Early prescriptions were often simple notes or verbal instructions, but with the advancement of medical knowledge and the proliferation of pharmaceuticals, the need for clear, written orders became evident. This evolution has led to the modern prescription format, which includes comprehensive details to prevent errors and ensure proper patient care.

Parts of a Prescription

Prescriber's Information

Including the prescriber's name, address, contact information, and qualifications is crucial. This information ensures accountability, allows for easy contact if there are questions about the prescription, and verifies the prescriber's authority. It also aids in tracking and managing patient care effectively, providing a point of reference for future consultations or treatments.

Patient's Information

Accurate patient details, including the patient's name, address, age, and gender, are essential to ensure the medication is provided to the correct individual and that the treatment is appropriate for the patient's demographic characteristics. This helps prevent medication errors and allows for personalized treatment. Additionally, patient history and any known allergies or medical conditions should be considered to avoid adverse reactions.

Date

The date on a prescription is important for several reasons. It provides a timeline for when the medication was prescribed, which is important for tracking the duration of treatment and ensuring that the medication is used within an appropriate time frame. It also helps in monitoring the prescription's validity and the timing of refills. In some cases, the date can influence the potency and shelf-life of the medication, making it a critical component of the prescription.

Rx Symbol

The Rx symbol, derived from the Latin word "recipe," meaning "take," is a traditional part of a prescription. Historically, it signifies a command to take the listed ingredients and prepare the medication. It is a universally recognized symbol in medical prescriptions, signifying the official nature of the document and the authority of the prescriber.

Medication Details

Drug Name

It's important to specify the drug name clearly, using generic names to avoid confusion and ensure the patient receives the correct medication. Generic names are preferred for their universality and cost-effectiveness compared to brand names. The use of generic names also reduces the risk of medication errors and ensures consistency in treatment across different healthcare providers and pharmacies.

Dosage Form

The form in which the drug is to be administered, such as tablet, capsule, or suspension, should be specified to ensure the correct preparation and administration method. Different dosage forms can have varying effects on the body's absorption and efficacy of the medication, making this information crucial for effective treatment.

Strength

Indicating the strength or concentration of the medication is critical to ensure the patient receives the correct dose. This detail helps avoid underdosing or overdosing, both of which can have serious health implications. The strength should be clearly stated in appropriate units (e.g., mg, mL) to avoid confusion.

Quantity

Specifying the total amount to be dispensed helps in managing the treatment duration and ensuring the patient has enough medication for the prescribed period. It also helps in preventing misuse or overuse of medication. Pharmacists use this information to ensure that the patient receives the exact amount needed for their treatment course.

Instructions for Use

Dosage Instructions

Properly writing dosage instructions helps avoid ambiguity and ensures the patient understands how much medication to take. Clear instructions reduce the risk of improper usage, which can lead to ineffective treatment or adverse effects. Dosage instructions should include the exact amount of medication to be taken at each interval.

Route of Administration

The route (e.g., oral, topical, intravenous) should be specified to ensure the medication is taken correctly and to avoid potential complications. Different routes can affect the drug's absorption and effectiveness. For instance, some medications are designed to be absorbed through the skin, while others are intended for direct injection into the bloodstream.

Frequency and Duration

Detailed guidance on how often and for how long the medication should be taken ensures the treatment is effective and minimizes the risk of side effects or resistance. This information helps patients adhere to the prescribed regimen and achieve the best possible outcomes from their treatment.

Additional Instructions

Special instructions, such as taking the medication with food, on an empty stomach, or at specific times of the day, can significantly affect the medication's effectiveness and patient compliance. These instructions help optimize the drug's absorption and minimize potential side effects.

Signature of the Prescriber

The prescriber's signature is a legal requirement that validates the prescription, confirming the authenticity and authorization by the healthcare professional. It is essential for legal and professional accountability. A signed prescription indicates that the prescriber has reviewed and approved the treatment plan.

Refill Information

Specifying the number of refills and the importance of this information helps manage long-term treatments, ensuring continuity of care without unnecessary interruptions. It also aids in monitoring medication usage and preventing overuse or misuse. Refill information ensures that patients can continue their treatment without repeated visits to the prescriber, promoting adherence and stable management of chronic conditions.

Handling Prescriptions

Receiving Prescriptions

Verification of Prescription Details

When a prescription is received, it's crucial to verify its accuracy and completeness to ensure patient safety. Steps to verify include:

- Checking for the prescriber's details, including their name, contact information, and qualifications.
- Ensuring the patient's information is complete and correct.
- Confirming the date of the prescription to ensure it is current.
- Verifying the medication details, including drug name, dosage form, strength, quantity, and instructions for use.
- Ensuring the prescriber's signature is present and valid.

Clarification with Prescriber

Pharmacists should contact the prescriber for clarification if:

- There are any unclear or illegible instructions.
- The prescribed dosage seems unusual or outside the standard therapeutic range.
- There are potential interactions with the patient's other medications.
- Additional patient information is required to safely dispense the medication.

Dispensing Medications

Reading and Interpreting Prescriptions

Pharmacists need to be trained in accurately interpreting prescriptions to ensure correct medication dispensing. This involves:

- Familiarity with common abbreviations and symbols used in prescriptions.
- Understanding dosage calculations and conversions.
- Recognizing potential drug interactions and contraindications.

Preparing Medications

Procedures for preparing medications include:

- Measuring and counting tablets or capsules accurately using calibrated tools.
- Ensuring the correct formulation (e.g., liquid, ointment) is prepared as per the prescription.
- Using aseptic techniques if preparing sterile medications.
- Double-checking the medication and dosage before packaging.

Labeling

Accurate and clear labeling is essential and should include:

- The patient's name and address.
- The drug name, dosage form, strength, and quantity.
- Clear usage instructions, including the route of administration, frequency, and duration.
- Any special instructions, such as taking with food or avoiding certain activities.
- Warnings about potential side effects or interactions.

Patient Counseling

Providing Usage Instructions

Pharmacists should use clear, non-technical language to explain how to use the medication. Techniques include:

- Demonstrating how to use devices (e.g., inhalers, insulin pens).
- Providing written instructions to supplement verbal explanations.
- Using visual aids or diagrams when necessary.

Adherence to Medication

Strategies to ensure patient adherence include:

- Explaining the importance of taking the medication as prescribed.
- Discussing the consequences of missed doses.
- Setting up reminder systems, such as medication calendars or alarms.

Addressing Patient Concerns

Pharmacists should be prepared to address common patient concerns, such as:

- Side effects and how to manage them.
- What to do if a dose is missed.
- Interactions with other medications or dietary restrictions.
- Ensuring privacy and a comfortable environment for patients to discuss their concerns openly.

Record-Keeping
Maintaining Prescription Records

Maintaining accurate and up-to-date prescription records is a legal and professional requirement for pharmacies. Key practices include:

- Keeping detailed records of all prescriptions dispensed, including the date, patient details, prescriber details, medication information, and dispensing pharmacist.
- Using electronic health records (EHR) systems to ensure accuracy and accessibility of prescription data.
- Retaining records for the legally mandated period, typically several years, as specified by regulatory authorities.
- Ensuring records are easily retrievable for audits, legal inquiries, or patient history reviews.

Confidentiality and Privacy

Protecting patient information is crucial in pharmacy practice. Steps to ensure confidentiality include:

- Following data protection regulations, such as HIPAA (Health Insurance Portability and Accountability Act) in the United States.
- Implementing secure systems for storing and accessing prescription records, both electronic and physical.

- Training staff on confidentiality policies and the importance of protecting patient information.
- Limiting access to prescription records to authorized personnel only.

In summary, the prescription process involves detailed and systematic steps to ensure patient safety, effective medication administration, and compliance with legal requirements. From writing and receiving prescriptions to dispensing medications and maintaining records, each step is crucial in delivering quality healthcare.

Common Errors in Prescriptions and Their Prevention

Common Errors in Prescriptions and Their Prevention

Prescription errors are a significant concern in healthcare, as they can lead to serious patient harm. Understanding the types, causes, and prevention strategies for these errors is essential for ensuring patient safety and improving the overall quality of care.

Types of Prescription Errors

Omissions

Omissions refer to errors where critical information is missing from the prescription. These errors can severely impact patient safety and the effectiveness of the treatment. Common omissions include:

- **Dosage Instructions**: Failure to specify the amount, frequency, or duration of medication use can lead to incorrect dosing, which may result in underdosing (ineffectiveness) or overdosing (toxicity).
- **Route of Administration**: Not indicating whether the medication should be taken orally, topically, intravenously, etc., can lead to incorrect administration and potentially harmful outcomes.

Illegibility

Poor handwriting or unclear instructions are a common source of prescription errors. Illegible prescriptions can lead to misinterpretation by the pharmacist, resulting in the dispensing of incorrect medications or dosages. Clear and legible writing is essential to prevent these errors.

Incorrect Dosage or Strength

Errors in the prescribed dosage or strength of the medication can lead to serious consequences. Underdosing may render the treatment ineffective, while overdosing can cause toxicity and adverse reactions. Such errors highlight the need for precise and accurate prescription writing.

Drug Interactions

Prescribing medications without considering potential interactions with other drugs the patient is taking can lead to adverse effects. Drug interactions can reduce the effectiveness of treatments or cause harmful side effects. Therefore, it is crucial to review the patient's medication history thoroughly.

Contraindications

Prescribing medications that are contraindicated for the patient's condition or due to other medications they are taking can lead to severe health risks. Contraindications must be carefully considered to avoid prescribing drugs that could exacerbate existing conditions or interact negatively with other treatments.

Causes of Prescription Errors

Human Factors

Human factors play a significant role in prescription errors. Common issues include:

- **Fatigue or Burnout**: Prescribers who are tired or experiencing burnout are more likely to make mistakes.
- **Distractions or Interruptions**: Interruptions during the prescribing process can lead to oversight and errors.
- **High Workload or Time Pressures**: High patient loads and time constraints can cause rushed decisions and errors in prescriptions.

Communication Issues

Effective communication is crucial in healthcare. Errors can arise from:

- **Poor Communication Between Healthcare Providers**: Incomplete or unclear communication can lead to misunderstandings and errors in prescribing.
- **Incomplete or Inaccurate Transfer of Patient Information**: Errors can occur if patient information is not accurately conveyed or documented during transitions of care.

Knowledge Deficits

Lack of knowledge or insufficient training can lead to errors. This includes:

- **Lack of Knowledge About Drug Interactions and Contraindications**: Prescribers may not be fully aware of all potential drug interactions or contraindications.
- **Inadequate Training or Continuing Education**: Without ongoing education and training, prescribers may not stay updated on best practices and new medications.

Prevention Strategies
Standardization of Prescriptions
Standardizing prescriptions can significantly reduce errors:

- **Using Standardized Prescription Forms**: These forms ensure that all necessary information is included and consistently formatted.
- **Implementing Electronic Prescribing Systems**: E-prescribing can reduce errors from illegibility and improve accuracy by providing standardized templates and automated checks.

Education and Training
Ongoing education and training for healthcare providers are essential:

- **Best Prescribing Practices**: Training on the latest best practices, including proper dosage calculations and patient-specific considerations.
- **Drug Interactions and Contraindications**: Regular updates and workshops on drug interactions, contraindications, and new medications.
- **Continuing Education**: Encouraging prescribers to engage in lifelong learning to stay current with medical advancements.

Double-Checking Systems
Implementing double-checking systems can prevent errors:

- **Pharmacist Verification**: Having pharmacists verify prescriptions before dispensing ensures an additional layer of safety.
- **Cross-Checking with Patient Records**: Verifying the prescription against the patient's medical records to catch potential errors.

Patient Involvement

Encouraging patient involvement can enhance safety:

- **Active Participation**: Patients should be encouraged to ask questions about their prescriptions and verify medications with the pharmacist.
- **Clear Instructions**: Providing clear, written instructions and information leaflets to help patients understand their medications and dosages.
- **Patient Education**: Educating patients on the importance of adherence to prescribed treatments and how to manage their medications.

Use of Technology

Leveraging technology can reduce prescription errors:

- **Electronic Health Records (EHR)**: EHR systems provide a comprehensive view of the patient's medical history, reducing errors due to incomplete information.
- **Computerized Physician Order Entry (CPOE)**: CPOE systems standardize the prescribing process and incorporate checks to prevent errors.
- **Drug Interaction Checkers and Clinical Decision Support Systems (CDSS)**: These tools help identify potential drug interactions and contraindications, providing real-time alerts to prescribers.

CHAPTER FOUR

Posology

Posology is the branch of medical science that deals with the determination of the doses of drugs and medications required to achieve the desired therapeutic effect. It involves calculating and prescribing the correct dosage to ensure that the medication is effective while minimizing the risk of adverse effects. This discipline is essential for optimizing drug therapy by tailoring doses to individual patient needs based on various factors.

Etymology

The term 'posology' is derived from the Greek words "posos," meaning "how much," and "logos," meaning "study." This origin reflects the core focus of posology, which is to study and determine the appropriate amount of medication needed for effective treatment. The historical roots of the term emphasize the importance of quantifying and understanding the necessary dosage for therapeutic success.

Scope of Posology

The scope of posology is broad and encompasses various aspects, including:

- **Determining Dosages for Different Age Groups**: Dosage requirements can vary significantly between children, adults, and the elderly due to differences in metabolism, organ function, and body composition. Posology provides guidelines for adjusting doses appropriately for each age group.
- **Adjusting Doses Based on Body Weight, Height, and Body Surface Area**: Individual physical characteristics such as weight and body surface area can influence drug absorption, distribution, metabolism, and excretion. Posology involves calculating doses that are proportional to

these factors to achieve optimal therapeutic levels.

- **Modifying Dosages for Patients with Specific Medical Conditions**: Conditions like renal or hepatic impairment can affect how drugs are processed in the body. Posology takes into account these medical conditions to adjust dosages and avoid potential toxicity or subtherapeutic effects.
- **Considering Pharmacokinetic and Pharmacodynamic Principles**: Understanding how drugs move through the body (pharmacokinetics) and how they exert their effects (pharmacodynamics) is crucial for determining the correct dose. Posology integrates these principles to tailor doses for optimal efficacy and safety.
- **Accounting for Genetic Factors**: Genetic variations can influence drug metabolism and response. Posology includes considerations of pharmacogenomics to personalize medication regimens based on genetic profiles, enhancing treatment effectiveness and reducing adverse reactions.

Importance of Posology

Therapeutic Efficacy

Correct dosages are crucial to ensure that treatments are effective. Administering the right dose ensures that the drug reaches the required concentration in the body to exert its therapeutic effect, thereby achieving the desired clinical outcomes. Proper dosing maximizes the drug's benefits and contributes to successful patient outcomes.

Safety Considerations

Posology plays a vital role in preventing overdoses and minimizing side effects. By determining the appropriate dose, healthcare providers can reduce the risk of drug toxicity and adverse reactions, which is especially important for medications with narrow therapeutic indices. This focus on safety helps protect patients from potentially harmful effects of medications.

Individualized Treatment

One of the key aspects of posology is its role in tailoring dosages to individual patient needs. Factors such as age, weight, gender, genetic makeup, and overall health status are taken into account to customize the dosage regimen. This individualized approach helps in maximizing the therapeutic benefits while minimizing potential risks. Personalized dosages ensure that each patient receives the most appropriate treatment for their specific condition and characteristics.

Regulatory Standards

Regulatory bodies like the Food and Drug Administration (FDA) and European Medicines Agency (EMA) set guidelines and standards for dosage determination to ensure patient safety and drug efficacy. These standards are based on extensive clinical trials and research, and adherence to these guidelines is essential for the approval and use of medications. Posology ensures compliance with these regulations, thus safeguarding public health. Following these regulatory standards helps maintain high quality and consistency in medication management, protecting patients and ensuring reliable therapeutic outcomes.

Additional Considerations in Posology

Clinical Trials and Research

Posology is grounded in rigorous clinical trials and research. These studies provide the data needed to determine safe and effective dosage ranges for various populations. Research in posology continues to evolve, incorporating new findings from pharmacology, genetics, and clinical practice to refine dosing recommendations.

Advances in Technology

Technological advancements, such as computerized dosing calculators and decision support systems, have enhanced the accuracy and precision of posology. These tools help healthcare providers determine the most appropriate doses quickly and accurately, reducing the likelihood of errors and improving patient care.

Multidisciplinary Approach

Posology often involves collaboration among various healthcare professionals, including pharmacists, physicians, and nurses. This multidisciplinary approach ensures that all aspects of a patient's health and treatment are considered when determining the appropriate dosage, leading to more comprehensive and effective care.

In summary, posology is a critical field in medical science focused on determining the appropriate doses of medications to achieve therapeutic goals while minimizing risks. Its broad scope includes considerations of age, weight, medical conditions, pharmacokinetics, pharmacodynamics, and genetics. By ensuring therapeutic efficacy, safety, individualized treatment, and compliance with regulatory standards, posology plays a vital role in optimizing patient care and improving health outcomes.

Factors Affecting Posology

Patient-Specific Factors

1. **Age**:

   - **Neonates and Infants**: Immature liver and kidney functions affect drug clearance, necessitating lower doses or extended dosing intervals. The development of these organs over time requires frequent dose adjustments.
   - **Elderly**: Decreased organ function, multiple comorbidities, and polypharmacy in the elderly necessitate careful dose adjustments to prevent toxicity. Age-related physiological changes like reduced renal and hepatic function can alter drug pharmacokinetics.

2. **Weight**:

   - Dosage calculations often take body weight into account to ensure accurate drug delivery. Pediatric doses and chemotherapeutic agents are commonly calculated based on mg/kg of body weight. This method helps achieve therapeutic efficacy without causing harm, as it considers the patient's size relative to the dose.

3. **Gender**:

   - Differences in body composition, hormone levels, and enzyme activity between genders can affect drug metabolism and response. For instance, females may have a higher percentage of body fat, influencing the distribution of lipophilic drugs. Hormonal variations can also alter drug efficacy and toxicity profiles, necessitating gender-specific dosage adjustments.

4. **Genetic Factors**:

   - Genetic variations can significantly impact drug metabolism and response. Pharmacogenetics studies these variations to tailor drug therapy to individual genetic profiles. For instance, certain genetic polymorphisms in cytochrome P450 enzymes can alter drug metabolism rates, requiring dose modifications to achieve optimal therapeutic outcomes.

Physiological and Pathological Factors

1. **Body Surface Area (BSA):**

   - BSA is particularly important in calculating doses for drugs with narrow therapeutic indices, such as chemotherapeutic agents. BSA-based dosing helps standardize doses across different body sizes, reducing the risk of toxicity and ensuring effective drug levels.

2. **Organ Function:**

   - **Liver Function:** Impaired hepatic function can lead to reduced metabolism of drugs, requiring dose reductions to prevent accumulation and toxicity.
   - **Kidney Function:** Renal impairment can decrease drug excretion, necessitating careful monitoring and dose adjustments to prevent drug toxicity.

3. **Pregnancy and Lactation:**

   - During pregnancy, physiological changes such as increased blood volume and altered organ function can affect drug pharmacokinetics, necessitating dose adjustments to ensure both maternal and fetal safety.
   - Lactating women require special considerations to prevent drug transfer through breast milk, potentially harming the infant.

Drug-Specific Factors

1. **Pharmacokinetics (ADME):**

   - **Absorption:** How a drug enters the bloodstream.
   - **Distribution:** How a drug spreads through the body's tissues.

- ○ **Metabolism**: How the drug is broken down, primarily in the liver.
- ○ **Excretion**: How the drug is eliminated from the body, mainly through the kidneys.

2. **Pharmacodynamics**:

- ○ The relationship between drug concentration and its effect, often depicted through dose-response curves, guides dosage decisions. This relationship helps in determining the optimal dose that achieves the desired effect with minimal toxicity.

3. **Formulation and Route of Administration**:

- ○ The formulation of a drug (e.g., tablet, injection) and its route of administration (e.g., oral, intravenous) significantly influence its absorption and bioavailability. For instance, intravenous administration delivers the drug directly into the bloodstream, requiring precise dosing to avoid toxicity, whereas oral administration involves first-pass metabolism, often necessitating higher doses.

External Factors

1. **Diet and Lifestyle**:

- ○ Diet, alcohol consumption, and smoking can alter drug metabolism and effectiveness. For example, grapefruit juice can inhibit cytochrome P450 enzymes, affecting drug metabolism. Alcohol can either induce or inhibit drug-metabolizing enzymes, while smoking can enhance the metabolism of certain drugs, requiring dose adjustments.

Pediatric Dose Calculations: Age, Body Weight, and Body Surface Area
Importance of Accurate Pediatric Dosing

1. **Sensitivity to Dosage**:

○ Children are more sensitive to dosage errors due to their developing organ systems and varying body compositions. Incorrect dosages can lead to either subtherapeutic effects or toxicities. For instance, immature liver and kidney functions in infants can slow down drug metabolism and excretion, increasing the risk of drug accumulation and toxicity.

2. **Developmental Considerations:**

○ As children grow, their metabolic rates, organ functions, and body compositions change, influencing how drugs are processed and their effects on the body. For example, neonates have higher water content and lower fat content, which can affect the distribution of drugs. As they age, these ratios shift, impacting how medications are dosed and metabolized.

Methods of Pediatric Dose Calculation

By Age:
Young's Rule:

- **Formula:**

Pediatric Dose=(Age in years / Age in years+12)×Adult Dose

- **Application:** Young's Rule is primarily used for children aged 1-12 years. This rule helps estimate a child's dose based on their age in relation to an adult dose.

Cowling's Rule:

- **Formula:**

Pediatric Dose=(Age in years+1 /24)×Adult Dose

- **Usage and Limitations:** Cowling's Rule is another age-based dosing method but is less commonly used than Young's Rule due to its limited application and the general preference for weight-based dosing in modern practice.

By Body Weight:
Clark's Rule:

- **Formula:**

Pediatric Dose=(Weight in pounds /150)×Adult dose
Example: If an adult dose is 200 mg and the child weighs 50 pounds, the pediatric dose would be:
(50 /150)×200=66.67 mg
Dosage per Kilogram:

- **Standard Method:**

Pediatric Dose=Dose per kg×Weight in kg

- This method is widely used due to its accuracy and adaptability to various pediatric weights.

By Body Surface Area (BSA):
Formula for BSA Calculation:

- **Formula: BSA (m^2)=√(Height (cm)×weight (kg)/3600**
- This formula accounts for both the child's height and weight, providing a more precise dosing calculation.

Practical Examples

Case Studies:

1. **Young's Rule:**

- • **Scenario:** A 6-year-old child requires a medication with an adult dose of 100 mg.
  - **Calculation:**

Pediatric Dose=(6 / 6+12)×100=(6/18)×100=33.33 mg

1. **Clark's Rule:**

- • **Scenario:** A 4-year-old child weighing 40 pounds needs a medication with an adult dose of 200 mg.
  - **Calculation:**

Pediatric Dose=(40 /150)×200=53.33 mg

CHAPTER FIVE

Pharmaceutical Calculations

Systems of Weights and Measures: Imperial and Metric

Historical Development and Usage

The historical development of weights and measures systems is crucial to understanding their adoption in pharmacy practices. The **Imperial system** of weights and measures, which originated in the British Empire, was widely used in many countries, including India, during the colonial period. The **Metric system**, on the other hand, was developed in France during the late 18th century and has since become the international standard for scientific and commercial use.

The **Imperial system** includes units such as pounds, ounces, grains, gallons, quarts, and pints, which were used for various measurements, including weight, volume, and length. In contrast, the **Metric system** is based on units of ten, making it simpler and more consistent. It includes units such as grams, kilograms, liters, and meters, which are used universally in scientific and industrial contexts.

Origin and Evolution of Imperial and Metric Systems

The **Imperial system** was officially defined in the British Weights and Measures Act of 1824, standardizing measurements across the British Empire. This system evolved from earlier systems of measurement used in Britain, including those of the Roman and medieval periods. Over time, the Imperial system was refined and expanded to include more specific units tailored to various applications, including trade, construction, and medicine.

The **Metric system** was developed during the French Revolution to create a universal and rational system of measurement based on natural constants. The Metric system's simplicity and precision led to its rapid adoption in scientific research and industry worldwide. The International System of Units (SI), established in 1960, further standardized the Metric system, ensuring its global acceptance and use.

Adoption in Pharmacy Practices

The adoption of the Metric system in pharmacy practices has been driven by the need for precision, consistency, and ease of use. The Metric system's base-10 structure allows for straightforward calculations and conversions, reducing the risk of errors in medication dosing and compounding. As a result, most countries, including India, have adopted the Metric system for pharmaceutical calculations and practices.

Pharmacists are required to be proficient in both the Imperial and Metric systems, particularly in regions where the Imperial system is still used. This dual knowledge ensures that pharmacists can accurately interpret prescriptions and convert measurements as needed, maintaining the safety and efficacy of pharmaceutical preparations.

Conversion Between Systems

Converting between the Imperial and Metric systems is a critical skill for pharmacists, as prescriptions and medical records may use either system. Conversion involves using specific factors to translate measurements from one system to another.

Conversion Factors and Methods

Common conversion factors between the Imperial and Metric systems include:

- 1 pound (lb) = 453.592 grams (g)
    1 ounce (oz) = 28.3495 grams (g)
    1 ounce (oz) = 29.5735 milliliters (mL)
    1 grain = 64.79891 milligrams (mg)
    1 gallon (gal) = 3.78541 liters (L)
    1 pint (pt) = 473.176 milliliters (mL)

Practical Applications in Pharmacy

Use in Prescription Compounding Pharmacists frequently use both systems when compounding medications. Accurate measurement and conversion are essential to ensure that patients receive the correct dosage. For instance, if a compounding formula is provided in grams, but the available ingredients are measured in ounces, the pharmacist must convert these measurements to ensure the precise amount of each ingredient is used.

Measurement in Pharmaceutical Manufacturing In pharmaceutical manufacturing, precise measurements are critical to ensuring product quality and consistency. The Metric system is predominantly used due to its simplicity and accuracy. Manufacturing processes often involve scaling up from small laboratory measurements to large production quantities, requiring accurate conversions and calculations.

Calculations Involving Percentage Solutions

Definitions and Basic Concepts

Percentage solutions are commonly used in pharmacy to express the concentration of a solute in a solvent. These solutions can be categorized based on weight/volume (% w/v), weight/weight (% w/w), and volume/volume (% v/v). Understanding these concepts is essential for accurate drug formulation, compounding, and dispensing.

Understanding Percent Weight/Volume (% w/v), Weight/Weight (% w/w), Volume/Volume (% v/v)

Percent Weight/Volume (% w/v):

- This represents the number of grams of solute in 100 milliliters of solution.
- For example, a 10% w/v solution means there are 10 grams of solute dissolved in 100 milliliters of solution.

Percent Weight/Weight (% w/w):

- This indicates the number of grams of solute in 100 grams of solution.
- For instance, a 5% w/w ointment contains 5 grams of active ingredient in every 100 grams of the ointment.

Percent Volume/Volume (% v/v):

- This denotes the number of milliliters of solute in 100 milliliters of solution.
- For example, a 20% v/v alcohol solution has 20 milliliters of alcohol in 100 milliliters of total solution.

Preparation of Percentage Solutions

Methods and Steps for Preparation:

1. **Weight/Volume (% w/v):**

   - Calculate the required amount of solute.
   - Measure the solute accurately using a balance.
   - Dissolve the solute in a portion of the solvent.
   - Transfer the solution to a volumetric flask and add solvent up to the desired final volume.

2. **Weight/Weight (% w/w):**

   - Determine the weight of the solute needed.
   - Weigh the solute and the solvent separately.
   - Mix the solute thoroughly with the solvent until a homogenous mixture is achieved.

3. **Volume/Volume (% v/v).**

   - Calculate the volume of solute required.
   - Measure the solute and solvent using appropriate volumetric equipment.
   - Combine the solute with the solvent and mix well to achieve a uniform solution.

   Practical Examples in Pharmacy
   Example 1: Preparing a 10% w/v Sodium Chloride Solution:

- To prepare 100 mL of a 10% w/v sodium chloride solution:

- Weigh 10 grams of sodium chloride.
- Dissolve the sodium chloride in about 80 mL of water.
- Transfer the solution to a 100 mL volumetric flask and add water up to the 100 mL mark.

Example 2: Preparing a 5% w/w Hydrocortisone Cream:

- To prepare 100 grams of a 5% w/w hydrocortisone cream:

  - Weigh 5 grams of hydrocortisone.
  - Add the hydrocortisone to 95 grams of cream base.
  - Mix thoroughly to ensure an even distribution of the active ingredient.

Applications in Pharmacy Practice

Role in Drug Formulation and Dispensing: Percentage solutions are critical in formulating and dispensing medications. Pharmacists must accurately prepare these solutions to ensure therapeutic efficacy and patient safety. For example, intravenous (IV) solutions, topical creams, and oral syrups often require precise percentage calculations to achieve the desired concentration of active ingredients.

Examples in Clinical and Hospital Pharmacy:

- **IV Solutions**: Preparing IV fluids like a 0.9% w/v sodium chloride solution (normal saline) involves dissolving 9 grams of sodium chloride in 1 liter of water.
- **Topical Preparations**: A 2% w/v lidocaine gel is made by dissolving 2 grams of lidocaine in 100 mL of gel base.
- **Oral Solutions**: A 15% v/v ethanol solution used as a solvent for tinctures involves mixing 15 mL of ethanol with enough water to make a final volume of 100 mL.

Alligation Methods

Introduction to Alligation

Alligation is a mathematical technique used in pharmacy to solve problems related to mixing solutions or substances of different concentrations to achieve a desired concentration. It is particularly useful when compounding medications, where pharmacists need to prepare a specific strength by combining two or more solutions of known strengths. Alligation is divided into two methods: alligation medial and alligation alternate.

Basic Principles and Uses

Alligation Medial

Alligation medial is used to find the average concentration of a mixture when the quantities and concentrations of the individual components are known. This method is useful for determining the overall concentration of a mixture.

Principles:

- Calculate the total quantity of the mixture by summing the quantities of all components.
- Calculate the total amount of active ingredient by multiplying the quantity of each component by its concentration.
- Divide the total amount of active ingredient by the total quantity of the mixture to obtain the average concentration.

Example: If a pharmacist mixes 100 mL of a 10% solution with 200 mL of a 5% solution, the average concentration can be calculated as follows:

1. Total quantity = 100 mL + 200 mL = 300 mL
2. Total amount of active ingredient = (100 mL * 10%) + (200 mL * 5%) = 10 mL + 10 mL = 20 mL
3. Average concentration = (Total amount of active ingredient) / (Total quantity) = 20 mL / 300 mL = 6.67%

Alligation Alternate

Alligation Alternate

Introduction to Alligation Alternate

Alligation alternate is a method used in pharmacy calculations to determine the quantities of two solutions with different concentrations that need to be mixed to achieve a desired concentration. This technique is particularly useful when a specific concentration is required, and the available solutions have concentrations that are higher and lower than the desired concentration. The method involves creating a visual representation called the alligation grid or tic-tac-toe method, which simplifies the calculation process.

Basic Principles and Uses

Principles:

1. **Identify the concentrations:**

   - Determine the concentrations of the two available solutions.
   - Identify the desired concentration of the final mixture.

2. **Set up the alligation grid:**

   - Place the higher concentration in the top left corner and the lower concentration in the bottom left corner.
   - Place the desired concentration in the middle.

3. **Calculate the differences:**

   - Subtract the desired concentration from the higher concentration.
   - Subtract the lower concentration from the desired concentration.
   - Write these differences on the opposite sides of the grid.

4. **Determine the ratio:**

   - The differences represent the parts of each solution needed.
   - The ratio of the two solutions is the inverse of the differences calculated.

5. **Calculate the required volumes:**

   - Use the ratio to determine the volumes of each solution needed to achieve the desired concentration.

   Example Calculation:

To prepare 500 mL of a 7% solution using a 10% solution and a 4% solution:

- **List the concentrations**:

  - High concentration (C1) = 10%
  - Low concentration (C2) = 4%
  - Desired concentration (Cd) – 7%

- **Set up the alligation grid**

  10% | 3 parts

  7% |

  4% | 3 parts

- **Calculate the differences**:

  - Difference between 10% and 7% = 10% - 7% = 3 parts
  - Difference between 7% and 4% = 7% - 4% = 3 parts

- **Determine the ratio**:

  - The ratio of the 10% solution to the 4% solution is 3:3, which simplifies to 1:1.

- **Calculate the required volumes**:

  - Since the total volume required is 500 mL and the ratio is 1:1, equal volumes of each solution are needed.
  - Volume of 10% solution = 500 mL / (1+1) = 250 mL
  - Volume of 4% solution = 500 mL / (1+1) = 250 mL

By mixing 250 mL of the 10% solution with 250 mL of the 4% solution, a 500 mL solution with a 7% concentration is obtained.

Practical Applications in Pharmacy

Compounding Medications: Pharmacists often use alligation alternate to prepare customized medications at specific strengths. For example, a pharmacist may need to prepare a topical ointment with a specific concentration of an active ingredient by mixing two ointments of different strengths.

IV Admixtures: Alligation alternate is used to calculate the appropriate volumes of stock solutions required to prepare intravenous (IV) fluids with specific concentrations. This ensures that patients receive the correct dosage of medication.

Nutritional Solutions: In the preparation of nutritional solutions, alligation alternate helps pharmacists to mix solutions with different nutrient concentrations to achieve the desired formulation for patient-specific dietary needs.

Formulation Adjustments and Mixing

Alligation alternate is especially useful when adjustments need to be made to existing formulations. It allows pharmacists to modify the strength of a solution or mixture by combining different concentrations, ensuring the desired therapeutic effect is achieved without compromising safety or efficacy.

In practice, this method is applied in various settings:

- **Hospital Pharmacies**: Preparing IV admixtures and parenteral nutrition solutions.
- **Compounding Pharmacies**: Creating customized topical preparations, oral suspensions, and other dosage forms.
- **Clinical Settings**: Adjusting the concentrations of medications to meet specific patient needs.

By mastering the alligation alternate method, pharmacists can ensure precise and effective medication preparation, enhancing patient care and therapeutic outcomes.

Proof Spirit Calculations

Definition and Significance

Proof spirit calculations are essential for determining the alcohol content in various solutions, which is crucial in both pharmaceutical and beverage industries. Proof strength is a measure of the alcohol (ethanol) content in a liquid, expressed in degrees proof. In many countries, the proof system is used to describe the strength of alcoholic beverages and medicinal tinctures. Understanding proof strength and being able to perform proof spirit calculations are important for ensuring the correct formulation and dosage of alcohol containing pharmaceutical preparations.

Understanding Proof Strength and Alcohol Content

Proof Strength:

- In the United States, proof strength is defined as twice the alcohol by volume (ABV) percentage. For example, a solution with 50% ABV is 100 proof.
- In the United Kingdom, proof spirit is defined differently, where 100 proof is equivalent to 57.15% ABV. This definition originated from the old practice of testing the flammability of gunpowder when soaked in the spirit.

Alcohol Content:

- The alcohol content of a solution is often expressed as a percentage by volume (% v/v). This indicates how much of the solution is pure ethanol.

Methods of Calculation

Proof spirit calculations involve determining the proof strength of a solution based on its alcohol content, or vice versa. The two primary methods are:

1. Calculating proof strength from alcohol content.
2. Calculating alcohol content from proof strength.

Step-by-Step Calculation Process

Method 1: Calculating Proof Strength from Alcohol Content (US System):

1. Determine the alcohol by volume (ABV) percentage of the solution.
2. Multiply the ABV by 2 to find the proof strength.

Proof Strength=ABV×2Proof Strength=ABV×2
Example:

- A solution has 40% ABV.
- Proof strength = 40% ×× 2 = 80 proof.

Method 2: Calculating Alcohol Content from Proof Strength (US System):

1. Determine the proof strength of the solution.
2. Divide the proof strength by 2 to find the ABV.

ABV=Proof Strength2ABV=2Proof Strength
Example:

- A solution is 100 proof.
- ABV = 100 ÷÷ 2 = 50%.

Practical Examples
Example 1: Calculating Proof Strength

- A pharmacist needs to determine the proof strength of a tincture with 25% ABV.
- Proof strength = 25% ×× 2 = 50 proof.

Example 2: Calculating Alcohol Content

- A medicinal solution is labeled as 150 proof.
- ABV = 150 ÷÷ 2 = 75%.

Examples and Problem-Solving Techniques
Example 3: Mixing Alcohol Solutions

- To prepare 500 mL of a 60 proof alcohol solution using a 90 proof alcohol and water, determine the volumes needed.

  1. Convert 60 proof to ABV: 60 ÷÷ 2 = 30%.
  2. Convert 90 proof to ABV: 90 ÷÷ 2 = 45%.

3. Use the alligation method to find the ratio of 45% alcohol to water (0% ABV).

Set up the alligation grid:

45% | 30 parts

30% |

0% | 15 parts

Ratio of 45% alcohol to water = 30:15 = 2:1.

Calculate volumes for 500 mL total solution:

- Volume of 45% alcohol = (2 parts / (2+1 parts)) $\times$ 500 mL = 333.33 mL.
- Volume of water = (1 part / (2+1 parts)) $\times$ 500 mL = 166.67 mL.

By mixing 333.33 mL of 45% alcohol with 166.67 mL of water, a 500 mL solution with 30% ABV (60 proof) is obtained.

Application in Pharmaceutical Preparations

Proof spirit calculations are critical in the preparation of various pharmaceutical products, such as tinctures, elixirs, and other alcohol-based solutions. Ensuring the correct alcohol content is essential for the stability, efficacy, and safety of these preparations.

Example in Pharmaceutical Preparations:

- **Tinctures:** A tincture is a concentrated herbal extract made by soaking herbs in alcohol. The strength of the tincture is often specified in proof. Pharmacists must calculate the correct proof to ensure the proper extraction and preservation of the active ingredients.
- **Elixirs:** These are clear, sweetened, hydro-alcoholic solutions intended for oral use. The alcohol content helps to solubilize the active ingredients and acts as a preservative. Accurate proof spirit calculations are necessary to formulate elixirs with the appropriate alcohol concentration.

Isotonic Solutions Based on Freezing Point and Molecular Weight

Concept of Isotonicity

Isotonicity refers to the property of a solution having the same osmotic pressure as a specific body fluid, such as blood or tears. Solutions that are isotonic with body fluids prevent cells from shrinking (crenation) or swelling (lysis) due to osmosis. Maintaining isotonicity is crucial in pharmaceutical formulations, particularly for solutions intended for parenteral (injected) or ophthalmic (eye) use.

Definition and Importance in Pharmacy

Definition: An isotonic solution has the same osmotic pressure as another solution, usually body fluids like blood plasma or tears. This means it has the same concentration of solutes per unit of solvent, preventing osmosis that could harm cells.

Importance in Pharmacy:

- Ensuring solutions are isotonic with body fluids is critical for patient safety and comfort.
- Isotonic solutions are essential for intravenous (IV) infusions, ensuring that the administered fluid does not cause red blood cells to swell or shrink.
- In ophthalmic solutions, isotonicity ensures that eye drops do not cause irritation or discomfort.
- Maintaining isotonicity in nasal and wound care solutions helps prevent cellular damage and enhances patient comfort.

Methods to Calculate Isotonic Solutions

There are two primary methods to calculate isotonic solutions: the Freezing Point Depression Method and the Molecular Weight Method.

Freezing Point Depression Method

Principle: The freezing point of a solution decreases as the concentration of solute increases. The freezing point of human blood plasma and tears is approximately -0.52°C. By comparing the freezing point depression of a solution to that of body fluids, pharmacists can determine its isotonicity.

Calculation Steps:

1. Determine the freezing point depression of the solution in question.
2. Compare this value to the freezing point depression of body fluids (-0.52°C).

3. Adjust the concentration of solute to match the freezing point depression of the solution to that of body fluids.

Example:

- To prepare an isotonic solution using sodium chloride (NaCl):

  - The freezing point depression of 1% NaCl solution is approximately -0.58°C.
  - Since -0.58°C is close to -0.52°C, adjusting the concentration slightly to achieve an exact match can make the solution isotonic.

Molecular Weight Method

Principle: This method involves calculating the amount of a solute needed to make a solution isotonic based on its molecular weight and the desired volume of the solution.

Calculation Steps:

1. Calculate the number of osmoles per liter (osmolarity) needed to make the solution isotonic with body fluids.
2. Determine the molecular weight of the solute.
3. Use the formula:

Weight of solute (g)=Osmolarity (osmoles/L)×Molecular Weight (g/mole)×Volume (L)Number of ions produced by dissociationWeight of solute (g)−Number of ions produced by dissociationOsmolarity (osmoles/L)×Molecular Weight (g/mole)×Volume (L)

Example:

- To prepare 1 liter of an isotonic solution using dextrose (glucose), with a molecular weight of 180 g/mol:

  - The osmolarity of an isotonic solution is approximately 0.285 osmoles/L.
  - Dextrose does not dissociate into ions, so the formula simplifies to:

Weight of dextrose (g)=0.285 osmoles/L×180 g/mole×1 L=51.3 gWeight of dextrose (g)=0.285osmoles/L×180g/mole×1L=51.3g

Thus, 51.3 grams of dextrose is needed to make 1 liter of an isotonic solution.

Practical Implications in Formulations

Use in Ophthalmic and Parenteral Solutions:

1. **Ophthalmic Solutions:**

   - Eye drops and solutions must be isotonic to prevent irritation, discomfort, and potential damage to the eye tissues.
   - Common solutes used to adjust isotonicity include sodium chloride and dextrose.

2. **Parenteral Solutions:**

   - IV fluids, including saline and dextrose solutions, must be isotonic to ensure they do not cause hemolysis or crenation of red blood cells.
   - Adjusting the isotonicity of parenteral solutions involves careful calculation to match the osmotic pressure of blood plasma.

Examples:

- **Normal Saline:** A 0.9% NaCl solution is isotonic with blood plasma and is commonly used for IV infusions.
- **Ringer's Lactate:** This solution contains sodium chloride, potassium chloride, calcium chloride, and sodium lactate, balanced to be isotonic with body fluids, often used in fluid resuscitation.

Maintaining isotonicity is essential for the safety and efficacy of pharmaceutical preparations intended for use in sensitive environments like the bloodstream and eyes. Understanding and applying methods such as the Freezing Point Depression Method and the Molecular Weight Method allow pharmacists to formulate isotonic solutions accurately, ensuring patient comfort and preventing cellular damage.

CHAPTER SIX

Powders

Basic Definition of Powders in Pharmacy

In pharmacy, powders are defined as finely divided solid particles. These particles can consist of a single drug or a mixture of drugs and other excipients. Powders are one of the oldest dosage forms used in medicine, valued for their versatility and ease of administration.

Understanding Powders in Pharmacy

Powders in pharmacy are utilized in various ways, including as the basis for other dosage forms (e.g., tablets, capsules), as topical applications, or as bulk powders for internal use. They can be administered through different routes, including oral, topical, inhalation, and others, depending on the nature of the powder and the intended use.

Types of Powders

Powders can be classified into different types based on their composition and intended use. The main types include simple powders, compound powders, and specialized powders.

Simple Powders

- **Definition**: These contain a single active ingredient without any additional substances.
- **Example**: A pure drug substance like acetaminophen powder.

Compound Powders

- **Definition**: These consist of two or more active ingredients, often mixed with diluents or other excipients.

- **Example**: A combination of aspirin, caffeine, and acetaminophen powder.

Specialized Powders

- **Dusting Powders**: Used for topical application to protect the skin and absorb moisture. Examples include talcum powder and antifungal powders.
- **Effervescent Powders**: Contain acid and carbonate components that react in the presence of water to release carbon dioxide, making the solution effervescent. Examples include effervescent aspirin.
- **Efflorescent Powders**: Contain water of hydration that can be released when the powder is exposed to dry conditions or heat. Examples include citric acid.
- **Hygroscopic Powders**: Absorb moisture from the air, which can affect their stability and flow properties. Examples include calcium chloride.
- **Eutectic Mixtures**: Two or more substances that form a liquid when mixed, often requiring special handling to prevent liquefaction. Examples include camphor and menthol mixtures.

Classification Based on Particle Size and Use

Powders can also be classified according to particle size and their specific applications in pharmacy. The particle size affects the dissolution rate, stability, and handling properties of the powder.

Fine Powders

- **Definition**: Powders with very small particle sizes, usually less than 100 microns.
- **Use**: Often used for inhalation powders, topical applications, or as intermediates in tablet and capsule formulations.
- **Example**: Powdered sugar or talcum powder.

Coarse Powders

- **Definition**: Powders with larger particle sizes, typically between 100 and 1000 microns.

- **Use**: Used in bulk powders for oral administration or as granules for reconstitution.
- **Example**: Granulated sugar.

Granular Powders

- **Definition**: Powders that have been processed into granules, which are larger aggregates of fine particles.
- **Use**: Often used in effervescent powders, granules for reconstitution, or as intermediates in the production of tablets.
- **Example**: Granulated effervescent salts.

Practical Considerations in Pharmacy

Formulation

When formulating powders, pharmacists must consider factors such as particle size distribution, flow properties, and compatibility of ingredients. This ensures that the final product is stable, efficacious, and easy to handle and administer.

Processing

The methods used to process powders, such as milling, sieving, and granulation, can significantly impact their quality and performance. Proper techniques are essential to achieve the desired particle size and consistency.

Stability

Powders must be protected from environmental factors like moisture, light, and air to maintain their stability. Appropriate packaging and storage conditions are crucial to prevent degradation and ensure a long shelf life.

Administration

The route of administration influences the formulation and packaging of powders. For instance, inhalation powders require precise particle sizes for effective delivery to the lungs, while topical powders need to adhere well to the skin without causing irritation.

Advantages and Disadvantages

Benefits of Powdered Dosage Forms

1. **Stability**

   - **Chemical Stability**: Powders often have greater chemical stability compared to liquid dosage forms because they lack water, which can catalyze hydrolysis and other degradation reactions. This extends the shelf life of the active ingredients.
   - **Physical Stability**: Powders are less likely to experience phase separation or precipitation compared to suspensions and emulsions. They are also less prone to microbial contamination due to the absence of water.

2. **Dosage Flexibility**

   - **Customizable Doses**: Powders allow for flexible dosing, as they can be easily measured and adjusted according to the patient's needs. This is particularly useful for pediatric and geriatric patients who may require doses different from standard tablet or capsule forms.
   - **Multiple Routes of Administration**: Powders can be administered orally, topically, inhalationally, or even used in reconstitution to form other dosage forms like suspensions and solutions.

3. **Ease of Administration**

   - **Simple to Use**: Powders are relatively easy to administer. They can be mixed with food or drinks, which is beneficial for patients who have difficulty swallowing pills.
   - **Rapid Absorption**: When administered orally, powders can dissolve quickly in the gastrointestinal fluids, leading to rapid onset of action compared to solid forms like tablets.

Limitations and Challenges

1. **Handling**

   - **Dusting and Loss**: Powders can be prone to dusting, which can lead to the loss of material during handling and administration. This can result in dosing inaccuracies and wastage.

- **Static Electricity**: Fine powders can develop static charges, causing them to adhere to surfaces and complicating handling and processing.

2. Palatability

- **Taste Masking**: Many drugs in powder form have a bitter or unpleasant taste, which can affect patient compliance. Taste-masking techniques, such as flavoring agents or coating the particles, may be necessary.
- **Texture**: The gritty texture of some powders can be unpalatable, especially for oral administration, requiring formulation adjustments to improve mouthfeel.

3. Hygroscopicity

- **Moisture Absorption**: Hygroscopic powders absorb moisture from the air, which can lead to clumping, degradation, or altered dissolution rates. This necessitates careful packaging and storage to protect the powder from humidity.
- **Storage Requirements**: Hygroscopic powders often require special storage conditions, such as desiccants in packaging and storage in cool, dry places, to maintain their stability and efficacy.

Official Preparations: Simple and Compound Powders
Simple Powders: Definitions and Examples
Definitions. Simple powders are pharmaceutical preparations containing only a single active ingredient without any additional excipients or diluents. These powders are prepared for specific therapeutic purposes where a pure substance is needed.

Examples:

- **Acetaminophen Powder**: Used for pain relief and fever reduction.
- **Ascorbic Acid Powder**: Used as a vitamin supplement.
- **Sodium Bicarbonate Powder**: Used as an antacid to relieve heartburn and indigestion.

Basic Composition and Uses:

- **Composition**: Simple powders consist solely of the active pharmaceutical ingredient (API) in its pure form.
- **Uses**: They are used when precise dosing of a single ingredient is required. They can be administered directly, mixed with food or drinks, or used as a base for compounding more complex formulations.

Compound Powders: Formulation and Uses

Formulation: Compound powders are pharmaceutical preparations containing two or more active ingredients. These powders may also include excipients to improve stability, taste, or solubility. The ingredients are accurately weighed and thoroughly mixed to ensure a homogeneous distribution of the active substances.

Examples:

- **Compound Analgesic Powder**: A mixture of acetaminophen, caffeine, and aspirin used for pain relief.
- **Antacid Powder**: A combination of calcium carbonate, magnesium hydroxide, and simethicone used to neutralize stomach acid and relieve gas.

Complex Preparations and Therapeutic Applications:

- **Complex Preparations**: Compound powders often require precise formulation techniques to ensure the correct ratios of active ingredients. They may also include flavoring agents to improve palatability.
- **Therapeutic Applications**: Compound powders are used for a variety of therapeutic purposes, including pain management, gastrointestinal relief, and nutritional supplementation. They are particularly useful in treating conditions that require a combination of medications for optimal efficacy.

Official Standards and Monographs

Reference to Pharmacopoeial Standards: Pharmacopoeial standards regulate the formulation and quality of simple and compound powders, such as those provided in the United States Pharmacopeia (USP), British Pharmacopoeia (BP), and Indian Pharmacopoeia (IP). These standards include detailed monographs that specify the identity, purity, strength, and quality of the powders.

Example of a Monograph:

- **Aspirin Powder:**

  - **Description**: White, crystalline powder.
  - **Purity**: Contains not less than 99.5% and not more than 100.5% of C9H8O4.
  - **Identification**: Infrared absorption spectrophotometry.
  - **Assay**: Titrimetric or chromatographic methods.
  - **Impurities**: Limits specified for related substances.
  - **Storage**: Store in a tightly closed container, protected from light and moisture.

Compliance with Standards: Ensuring that pharmaceutical powders comply with these standards is crucial for their safety and efficacy. Pharmacists must adhere to these guidelines during formulation, compounding, and quality control processes.

Specialized Powders

Dusting Powders: Composition and Uses

Composition: Dusting powders are finely divided powders intended for external use on the skin. They typically contain absorbent substances, antiseptics, and/or lubricants. Common ingredients include talc, zinc oxide, starch, and kaolin. Antiseptic agents such as boric acid or salicylic acid may also be included to prevent infections.

Uses: Dusting powders are used to protect the skin, absorb moisture, reduce friction, and prevent infections. They are commonly applied to areas prone to irritation and moisture, such as feet, armpits, and the perineal region.

Application in Dermatology: In dermatology, dusting powders treat conditions like diaper rash, athlete's foot, and intertrigo. They help to keep the skin dry and reduce irritation caused by friction and moisture.

Effervescent Powders: Preparation and Applications

Preparation: Effervescent powders contain acid (e.g., citric acid or tartaric acid) and carbonate or bicarbonate salts (e.g., sodium bicarbonate). When mixed with water, they react to release carbon dioxide, creating effervescence. The ingredients must be mixed in dry conditions to prevent premature reactions.

Formulation Techniques: The ingredients are finely powdered and then blended uniformly. Granulation may be performed to improve flow properties and prevent segregation. They are typically packaged in moisture-resistant containers to maintain stability.

Examples:

- **Effervescent Vitamin C**: Used as a dietary supplement.
- **Effervescent Aspirin**: Used for pain relief and to reduce fever.

Applications: Effervescent powders are used for oral administration, providing a palatable and easy-to-dissolve dosage form. They enhance the absorption of certain medications by creating a buffered solution.

Efflorescent Powders: Handling and Storage

Characteristics: Efflorescent powders contain water of hydration that can be released in dry conditions, causing the powder to become pasty or liquid. Examples include sodium sulfate decahydrate and citric acid monohydrate.

Challenges: Efflorescence can affect the stability and efficacy of the powder, complicating handling and storage.

Management Strategies: Store efflorescent powders in airtight containers to prevent the loss of water of hydration. Use desiccants in packaging to absorb excess moisture and maintain the integrity of the powder.

Hygroscopic Powders: Characteristics and Management

Characteristics: Hygroscopic powders absorb moisture from the air, which can lead to clumping, degradation, or altered dissolution rates. Common examples include calcium chloride and magnesium sulfate.

Prevention of Moisture Absorption: Store hygroscopic powders in tightly sealed containers with desiccants to absorb moisture. Use moisture-resistant packaging materials, such as glass or plastic with moisture barriers. Handle these powders in low-humidity environments to minimize moisture exposure.

Eutectic Mixtures: Formation and Implications

Formation: Eutectic mixtures are formed when two or more substances are mixed and they liquefy at a lower temperature than their individual melting points. Examples include mixtures of camphor and menthol or thymol and chloral hydrate.

Implications: The liquefaction can complicate the handling and formulation of these powders, affecting their stability and usability.

Handling and Use in Formulations: Store eutectic mixtures in cool, dry places to prevent liquefaction. When compounding, mix each component with an inert absorbent like lactose or kaolin to separate the particles and prevent liquefaction. Use appropriate excipients to stabilize the mixture and maintain its physical form.

Geometric Dilutions

Concept and Importance: Geometric Dilution is a method used in pharmacy to ensure the even distribution of a small amount of a potent drug throughout a larger amount of diluent or base. It is particularly important when the drug is very potent and must be uniformly distributed to ensure accurate dosing. The importance of geometric dilution lies in its ability to achieve a homogeneous mixture, which is crucial for ensuring that each dose contains the same amount of active ingredient. This uniformity is essential for maintaining the efficacy and safety of the medication.

Role in Uniform Mixing: Geometric dilution ensures that a potent drug is evenly distributed throughout the mixture, preventing "hot spots" (areas with a high concentration of the drug) and "cold spots" (areas with little to no drug). This is critical in ensuring consistent therapeutic effects and avoiding potential overdoses or subtherapeutic doses.

Step-by-Step Process:

1. **Initial Mixing**:

   - Take the total amount of the drug to be diluted and place it in a suitable mixing vessel.
   - Add an approximately equal amount of the diluent to the potent drug. This initial step should ensure that the drug is adequately mixed with the diluent.

2. **First Dilution**:

   - Mix the drug and diluent thoroughly using a method that ensures even distribution, such as trituration with a mortar and pestle.
   - After the initial mixing, add an amount of diluent that is equal to the total amount already present in the mixture. For example, if you started with 1 gram of drug and added 1 gram of diluent, you would

now have 2 grams total. Add another 2 grams of diluent.

3. **Subsequent Dilutions**:

   ◦ Continue this process of adding an amount of diluent equal to the current total mixture and mixing thoroughly until all of the diluent has been added and the desired final concentration is achieved.

Practical Methodology: The key to effective geometric dilution is to ensure thorough and consistent mixing at each step. Using tools like a mortar and pestle can help achieve this, but mechanical mixers or blenders may be used for larger batches.

Practical Examples:

1. **Example 1**:

   ◦ To mix 1 gram of a potent drug with 9 grams of diluent:

     ▪ Mix 1 gram of drug with 1 gram of diluent (total = 2 grams).
     ▪ Add 2 grams of diluent to the 2 grams mixture (total = 4 grams).
     ▪ Add 4 grams of diluent to the 4 grams mixture (total = 8 grams).
     ▪ Add the remaining 1 gram of diluent to the 8 grams mixture (total = 9 grams).

2. **Example 2**:

   ◦ To mix 0.5 grams of a potent drug with 14.5 grams of diluent:

     ▪ Mix 0.5 grams of drug with 0.5 grams of diluent (total = 1 gram).
     ▪ Add 1 gram of diluent to the 1 gram mixture (total = 2 grams).
     ▪ Add 2 grams of diluent to the 2 grams mixture (total = 4 grams).
     ▪ Add 4 grams of diluent to the 4 grams mixture (total = 8 grams).
     ▪ Add the remaining 6.5 grams of diluent to the 8 grams mixture (total = 14.5 grams).

Applications and Relevance: Geometric dilution is widely used in pharmaceutical compounding, particularly for the preparation of dosage forms like capsules, tablets, and bulk powders. It is also relevant in the preparation of veterinary medicines, where accurate dosing is critical due to the varying sizes and weights of animals.

CHAPTER SEVEN

Liquid Dosage Forms

Liquid Dosage Forms in Pharmaceutical Practice

Liquid dosage forms are a fundamental category of pharmaceuticals, characterized by their administration in liquid states. They encompass a wide range of products, including solutions, suspensions, emulsions, and elixirs. These forms are essential in delivering therapeutic agents efficiently and effectively across various patient populations and medical conditions. Their versatility, ease of administration, and rapid onset of action make them indispensable in both clinical and at-home settings.

Importance and Benefits of Liquid Dosage Forms

Liquid dosage forms offer several significant benefits over their solid counterparts, enhancing patient compliance and therapeutic outcomes. Key advantages include:

1. **Ease of Swallowing:**

   - **Patient-Friendly:** Particularly advantageous for patients who have difficulty swallowing tablets or capsules, such as children, elderly individuals, and patients with dysphagia (difficulty swallowing).
   - **Flexible Administration:** Can be administered via various routes, including oral, topical, and parenteral, making them versatile for different medical conditions and patient needs.

2. **Rapid Absorption:**

- **Quick Onset of Action:** Generally have faster absorption rates compared to solid forms because the drug is already in a dissolved state, allowing for quicker onset of therapeutic effects. This is particularly beneficial for acute conditions requiring prompt relief, such as pain or fever.
- **Improved Bioavailability:** Enhance the bioavailability of certain drugs, ensuring that a higher proportion of the drug reaches systemic circulation and exerts its therapeutic effect.

3. **Dose Flexibility:**

- **Adjustable Dosing:** Allow for precise and flexible dosing. This is crucial for tailoring doses to individual patient needs, especially in populations requiring specific dose adjustments, such as pediatrics or geriatrics.
- **Ease of Mixing:** Enable the easy mixing of multiple drugs in a single formulation, simplifying the medication regimen and improving patient compliance.

Limitations and Considerations

Despite their many benefits, liquid dosage forms also present certain challenges and limitations that need to be addressed:

1. **Stability:**

- **Chemical Stability:** Can be less chemically stable than solid forms, as the presence of water can promote hydrolysis and other degradation reactions. This necessitates careful formulation to ensure drug stability over its shelf life.
- **Microbial Growth:** More prone to microbial contamination, requiring the addition of preservatives to prevent the growth of bacteria, fungi, and other pathogens.

2. **Storage:**

- **Special Requirements:** Often require specific storage conditions to maintain their stability and efficacy. For example, some may need refrigeration or protection from light to prevent degradation.
- **Packaging:** Often require specialized packaging, such as bottles with child-resistant caps, to ensure safety and maintain the integrity of the product.

3. **Patient Compliance:**

- **Taste and Palatability:** The taste of liquid medications can be a significant factor in patient compliance. Unpleasant flavors may lead to poor adherence, especially in pediatric patients. Flavoring agents and sweeteners are often added to improve palatability.
- **Measuring Accuracy:** Accurate dosing can be challenging with liquid forms, as patients need to measure doses correctly using droppers, syringes, or measuring cups. Inaccurate measurement can lead to underdosing or overdosing.

Solubility Enhancement Techniques

Importance of Solubility in Liquid Dosage Forms

Solubility is a critical factor in the formulation of liquid dosage forms because it directly impacts the drug's bioavailability and therapeutic efficacy. Poorly soluble drugs often have limited absorption in the gastrointestinal tract, leading to suboptimal therapeutic outcomes. Enhancing the solubility of these drugs can improve their dissolution rate, absorption, and overall bioavailability.

1. **Impact on Bioavailability and Efficacy:**

- **Bioavailability:** The extent and rate at which the active drug ingredient is absorbed from a dosage form and becomes available at the site of action. Enhanced solubility increases the concentration of the drug in the gastrointestinal fluids, leading to improved absorption and higher bioavailability.
- **Efficacy:** Higher solubility ensures that a sufficient amount of the drug reaches systemic circulation, thereby improving its therapeutic

efficacy. This is particularly important for drugs with poor water solubility, which might otherwise exhibit limited effectiveness.

Techniques to Enhance Solubility

Several techniques are employed to enhance the solubility of poorly soluble drugs in liquid dosage forms. These include the use of solvents and co-solvents, surfactants and solubilizing agents, and pH adjustment.

1. **Use of Solvents and Co-Solvents:**

    - **Solvents:** Solvents like water, ethanol, glycerin, and propylene glycol are commonly used in liquid formulations to dissolve the active pharmaceutical ingredient (API).
    - **Co-Solvents:** Co-solvents are added to improve the solubility of the drug in the primary solvent. Examples include ethanol, propylene glycol, polyethylene glycol (PEG), and glycerin.
    - **Mechanism:** Co-solvents work by reducing the interfacial tension between the hydrophobic drug and the aqueous solvent, thereby enhancing solubility.
    - **Example:** The solubility of diazepam can be significantly increased using ethanol and propylene glycol as co-solvents.

2. **Surfactants and Solubilizing Agents:**

    - **Surfactants:** Compounds that lower the surface tension between two liquids or a liquid and a solid. They form micelles that encapsulate the hydrophobic drug, increasing its solubility in aqueous solutions. Common surfactants include polysorbates (e.g., Tween 80), sorbitan esters, and sodium lauryl sulfate.
    - **Solubilizing Agents:** Agents such as cyclodextrins can form inclusion complexes with hydrophobic drugs, enhancing their solubility.
    - **Mechanism:** Surfactants and solubilizing agents work by increasing the solubility of the drug in the solvent, often through micelle formation or complexation.
    - **Example:** The solubility of poorly soluble drugs like itraconazole can be enhanced using cyclodextrins or polysorbates.

3. **pH Adjustment:**

- ○ **pH Adjustment:** Adjusting the pH of the solution can significantly enhance the solubility of ionizable drugs. By altering the pH, the drug can be converted into its more soluble ionized form.
- ○ **Buffers:** Buffers are often used to maintain the pH at a desired level, ensuring consistent solubility throughout the shelf life of the product.
- ○ **Example:** The solubility of weakly acidic drugs like aspirin can be increased by formulating them at a higher pH, where they exist in their ionized form.

Practical Applications and Case Studies

Example 1: Solvent and Co-Solvent System

- **Drug:** Phenytoin
- **Technique:** Use of propylene glycol and ethanol as co-solvents to enhance solubility in an oral liquid formulation.
- **Outcome:** Improved bioavailability and patient compliance due to the effective solubilization of the drug.

Example 2: Surfactant System

- **Drug:** Paclitaxel
- **Technique:** Formulation with Cremophor EL (a surfactant) to increase solubility in an injectable solution.
- **Outcome:** Enhanced solubility allowed for effective intravenous administration, improving therapeutic outcomes in cancer treatment.

Example 3: pH Adjustment

- **Drug:** Ibuprofen
- **Technique:** Formulating ibuprofen in a solution with adjusted pH to increase its solubility.
- **Outcome:** Enhanced solubility and faster onset of action in an oral liquid formulation.

Examples from Pharmaceutical Industry

Example 1: Ciprofloxacin Oral Solution

- **Technique:** Use of hydrochloric acid to adjust the pH and increase the solubility of ciprofloxacin in an oral solution.
- **Outcome:** Improved solubility and bioavailability, ensuring effective treatment of bacterial infections.

Example 2: Indomethacin Suspension

- **Technique:** Use of polysorbate 80 (a surfactant) to enhance the solubility of indomethacin in an oral suspension.
- **Outcome:** Increased solubility and improved patient compliance due to the better-tasting formulation.

Example 3: Amphotericin B Liposomal Injection

- **Technique:** Use of liposomal encapsulation to enhance the solubility and reduce the toxicity of amphotericin B.
- **Outcome:** Enhanced solubility, improved therapeutic index, and reduced side effects, leading to more effective treatment of fungal infections.

CHAPTER EIGHT

Monophasic Liquids

Monophasic Liquids are pharmaceutical preparations that consist of a single-phase system, where the solute is completely dissolved in the solvent, forming a homogeneous solution. These solutions are clear and uniform, with no visible particles or immiscible phases. Monophasic liquids are widely used in pharmaceutical formulations due to their simplicity, ease of administration, and quick onset of action.

Characteristics:

- **Homogeneous**: The solute is completely dissolved in the solvent, resulting in a clear, single-phase solution.
- **No Sedimentation**: Unlike suspensions, monophasic liquids do not require shaking before use, as there is no sedimentation of particles.
- **Uniform Dosage**: Each dose of a monophasic liquid contains an equal amount of the active ingredient, ensuring consistent therapeutic effects.

Common Types of Monophasic Liquids:

- **Syrups**: Concentrated aqueous solutions of sugar, often containing medicinal substances.
- **Elixirs**: Clear, sweetened hydro-alcoholic solutions intended for oral use.
- **Tinctures**: Alcoholic or hydro-alcoholic solutions of plant extracts or other medicinal substances.
- **Aromatic Waters**: Solutions of volatile oils or other aromatic substances in water.
- **Mouthwashes**: Solutions used for oral hygiene and therapeutic purposes.

Preparation of Monophasic Liquids

The preparation of monophasic liquids involves dissolving the solute(s) in the appropriate solvent(s) to achieve a clear, homogeneous solution. The following steps outline the general process for preparing monophasic liquids:

1. **Selection of Ingredients:**

   - **Active Ingredient**: Choose the active pharmaceutical ingredient (API) that will provide the desired therapeutic effect.
   - **Solvent**: Select an appropriate solvent that can dissolve the API. Common solvents include water, alcohol, glycerin, and propylene glycol.
   - **Excipients**: Additives such as preservatives, flavoring agents, sweeteners, and stabilizers may be included to enhance the formulation's stability, taste, and patient acceptability.

2. **Dissolution of Solute:**

   - **Weighing**: Accurately weigh the required amount of the API and other excipients.
   - **Dissolving**: Gradually add the API and excipients to the solvent while stirring continuously to ensure complete dissolution. This can be done at room temperature or with gentle heating if necessary to facilitate the dissolution process.

3. **Filtration:**

   - **Clarity**: Filter the solution to remove any undissolved particles or impurities, ensuring the final product is clear and homogeneous. Filtration can be done using appropriate filter media such as filter paper or membrane filters.

4. **Mixing and Homogenization:**

   - **Uniformity**: Thoroughly mix the filtered solution to ensure uniform distribution of all components. Homogenization may be required for some formulations to achieve a consistent solution.

5. **Quality Control**:

- **Testing**: Perform quality control tests to verify the solution's concentration, pH, clarity, and absence of particulate matter. These tests ensure the product meets specified standards and regulatory requirements.

6. **Packaging**:

- **Containers**: Package the monophasic liquid in suitable containers that protect it from light, moisture, and contamination. Common packaging options include glass or plastic bottles with appropriate closures.
- **Labeling**: Label the containers with essential information such as the product name, concentration, usage instructions, storage conditions, and expiration date.

Example:

- **Preparation of a Simple Syrup**:

  - **Ingredients**: Sucrose (850 g), Purified Water (450 mL)
  - **Procedure**: Dissolve sucrose in purified water by heating gently and stirring continuously until completely dissolved. Filter the solution to remove any impurities, then cool and package in clean, dry bottles.

Monophasic liquids are a fundamental dosage form in pharmacy, offering advantages such as ease of administration, rapid absorption, and uniform dosing. Understanding the definition, characteristics, and preparation methods of monophasic liquids is essential for pharmacists to ensure the safe and effective delivery of therapeutic agents.

Single-Phase Systems in Liquid Dosage Forms

Definition and Characteristics
   Single-Phase Systems:

- A single-phase system in liquid dosage forms refers to a homogeneous mixture where the solute is completely dissolved in the solvent, resulting in a clear and uniform solution. There are no distinct phases, particles, or immiscible components visible within the solution.

Characteristics:

- **Homogeneity**: The solution is consistent throughout, with the solute evenly distributed in the solvent.
- **Clarity**: Single-phase systems are typically clear and transparent, indicating the complete dissolution of the solute.
- **Stability**: These systems are generally stable, with no tendency for the solute to precipitate out of the solution under normal conditions.
- **Ease of Use**: Single-phase liquid dosage forms do not require shaking or agitation before use, as the solute remains uniformly distributed.

Common Types of Single-Phase Liquid Dosage Forms

1. **Syrups:**

   - **Definition**: Concentrated aqueous solutions of sugar, often containing medicinal substances and flavoring agents.
   - **Uses**: Commonly used for oral administration of medications, particularly for children due to their sweet taste.
   - **Example**: Cough syrups containing active ingredients like dextromethorphan or guaifenesin.

2. **Elixirs:**

   - **Definition**: Clear, sweetened hydro-alcoholic solutions intended for oral use, containing one or more active ingredients.
   - **Uses**: Used for medications that require both an aqueous and alcohol-based solvent to remain dissolved.
   - **Example**: Phenobarbital elixir used as an anticonvulsant.

3. **Tinctures:**

- **Definition**: Alcoholic or hydro-alcoholic solutions of plant extracts or other medicinal substances.
- **Uses**: Often used for herbal preparations and extracts.
- **Example**: Iodine tincture used as an antiseptic.

4. **Aromatic Waters**:

- **Definition**: Solutions of volatile oils or other aromatic substances in water.
- **Uses**: Used for their flavoring properties and mild therapeutic effects.
- **Example**: Peppermint water used to soothe digestive issues.

5. **Mouthwashes**:

- **Definition**: Solutions used for oral hygiene and therapeutic purposes, typically containing antiseptic, astringent, and deodorizing agents.
- **Uses**: Used to reduce oral bacteria, freshen breath, and promote oral health.
- **Example**: Chlorhexidine mouthwash used to reduce oral bacteria and prevent gingivitis.

Preparation of Single-Phase Systems

General Steps:

1. **Selection of Solvent and Solute**:

- Choose the appropriate solvent that can dissolve the active ingredient(s). Common solvents include water, alcohol, glycerin, and propylene glycol.

2. **Dissolution**:

- Accurately weigh the required amount of solute and gradually add it to the solvent with continuous stirring to ensure complete dissolution.

3. **Filtration:**

- Filter the solution to remove any undissolved particles or impurities, ensuring the final product is clear and homogeneous.

4. **Mixing and Homogenization:**

- Thoroughly mix the filtered solution to ensure uniform distribution of all components.

5. **Quality Control:**

- Perform quality control tests to verify the solution's concentration, pH, clarity, and absence of particulate matter.

6. **Packaging and Labeling:**

- Package the monophasic liquid in suitable containers that protect it from light, moisture, and contamination. Label the containers with essential information such as product name, concentration, usage instructions, storage conditions, and expiration date.

Examples of Single-Phase Systems in Liquid Dosage Forms

Example 1: Oral Syrup Preparation

- **Ingredients**: Paracetamol (120 mg), Sucrose (850 g), Purified Water (450 mL)
- **Procedure**: Dissolve paracetamol in a portion of purified water with gentle heating. Add sucrose and continue stirring until completely dissolved. Filter the solution, cool it, and then package it in bottles.

Example 2: Tincture Preparation

- **Ingredients**: Plant extract (ginseng), Ethanol (70%), Purified Water

- **Procedure**: Macerate the plant extract in ethanol for a specified period. Filter the solution, add purified water to reach the desired volume and alcohol concentration, then package in amber glass bottles to protect from light.

General Preparation Methods for Monophasic Liquid Dosage Forms

General Preparation Methods

The preparation of monophasic liquid dosage forms involves a series of systematic steps to ensure that the final product is homogeneous, stable, and effective. These methods ensure that the active pharmaceutical ingredients (APIs) and excipients are thoroughly dissolved in the solvent, resulting in a clear and consistent solution.

Step-by-Step Process for General Preparation Methods

1. **Selection of Ingredients:**

   - **Active Ingredient (API)**: Choose the appropriate API based on the therapeutic goal.
   - **Solvent**: Select a suitable solvent that can effectively dissolve the API. Common solvents include water, ethanol, glycerin, and propylene glycol.
   - **Excipients**: Additives such as preservatives, sweeteners, flavoring agents, stabilizers, and buffering agents may be included to enhance the formulation's stability, taste, and patient acceptability.

2. **Weighing and Measuring:**

   - Accurately weigh the required amount of the API and excipients.
   - Measure the volume of the solvent to ensure precise formulation.

3. **Dissolution:**

   - **API Dissolution**: Gradually add the API to the solvent while continuously stirring to promote complete dissolution. This can be done at room temperature or with gentle heating if necessary.

- **Excipient Addition**: Add excipients such as preservatives and flavoring agents to the solution and continue stirring until fully dissolved.

4. **Filtration**:

   - Filter the solution to remove any undissolved particles or impurities. Filtration ensures that the final product is clear and homogeneous.
   - **Filter Types**: Use appropriate filter media such as filter paper or membrane filters depending on the nature of the solution and the particle size to be removed.

5. **Mixing and Homogenization**:

   - After filtration, thoroughly mix the solution to ensure uniform distribution of all components. Homogenization may be required for certain formulations to achieve a consistent solution.

6. **Quality Control**:

   - Perform quality control tests to verify the solution's concentration, pH, clarity, and absence of particulate matter. These tests ensure that the product meets specified standards and regulatory requirements.

7. **Packaging**:

   - **Container Selection**: Package the monophasic liquid in suitable containers that protect it from light, moisture, and contamination. Common packaging options include glass or plastic bottles with appropriate closures.
   - **Labeling**: Label the containers with essential information such as product name, concentration, usage instructions, storage conditions, and expiration date.

Example Preparation Methods for Different Monophasic Liquid Dosage Forms
1. Syrups
Ingredients:

- API (e.g., Paracetamol)
- Sucrose
- Purified Water
- Preservatives (e.g., methylparaben)
- Flavoring agents (e.g., cherry flavor)

Procedure:

1. Dissolve the API in a portion of purified water with gentle heating.
2. Add sucrose to the solution and continue stirring until completely dissolved.
3. Add preservatives and flavoring agents, ensuring they are fully dissolved.
4. Filter the solution to remove any impurities.
5. Cool the solution to room temperature and package in clean, dry bottles.

2. Elixirs
Ingredients:

- API (e.g., Phenobarbital)
- Ethanol
- Glycerin
- Purified Water
- Sweeteners (e.g., sorbitol)
- Flavoring agents (e.g., vanilla extract)

Procedure:

1. Dissolve the API in ethanol.
2. Add glycerin and mix thoroughly.
3. Add purified water and sweeteners to the mixture.
4. Add flavoring agents and ensure complete dissolution.
5. Filter the solution to ensure clarity.
6. Package the elixir in amber glass bottles to protect from light.

3. Tinctures
Ingredients:

- Plant extract (e.g., Ginseng)

- Ethanol (70%)
- Purified Water

Procedure:

1. Macerate the plant extract in ethanol for a specified period (e.g., 14 days).
2. Filter the macerated solution to remove solid plant material.
3. Dilute the filtered solution with purified water to achieve the desired alcohol concentration.
4. Package the tincture in amber glass bottles to protect from light.

4. Aromatic Waters
Ingredients:

- Volatile oil (e.g., Peppermint oil)
- Purified Water

Procedure:

1. Dissolve the volatile oil in purified water with continuous stirring.
2. Allow the solution to stand for a specified period to let any undissolved particles settle.
3. Filter the solution to ensure clarity and remove any undissolved particles.
4. Package the aromatic water in glass bottles to preserve the aroma and efficacy.

5. Mouthwashes
Ingredients:

- Antiseptic agent (e.g., Chlorhexidine gluconate)
- Astringent (e.g., Zinc chloride)
- Flavoring agents (e.g., mint flavor)
- Purified Water

Procedure:

1. Dissolve the antiseptic agent and astringent in purified water with continuous stirring.
2. Add flavoring agents and ensure complete dissolution.
3. Filter the solution to remove any undissolved particles.
4. Package the mouthwash in plastic or glass bottles with appropriate closures.

Techniques and Equipment Used in the Preparation of Monophasic Liquid Dosage Forms

The preparation of monophasic liquid dosage forms requires a combination of techniques and specialized equipment to ensure the proper dissolution, mixing, and filtration of ingredients. Below is an overview of the key techniques and equipment commonly used in the preparation of these pharmaceutical formulations.

Techniques

1. Dissolution

- **Technique**: Dissolution involves dissolving the active pharmaceutical ingredient (API) and excipients in a suitable solvent to create a homogeneous solution.
- **Steps**:

  - Weigh the required amounts of API and excipients.
  - Add the API and excipients to the solvent gradually while stirring continuously to ensure complete dissolution.
  - Gentle heating may be used to facilitate dissolution if the solute has low solubility at room temperature.

2. Filtration

- **Technique**: Filtration is used to remove undissolved particles, impurities, or contaminants from the solution, ensuring clarity and homogeneity.
- **Steps**:

- Pass the solution through an appropriate filter medium (e.g., filter paper, membrane filters) to separate solid particles.
- Ensure the filtration process does not alter the concentration or stability of the solution.

3. Mixing and Homogenization

- **Technique**: Mixing and homogenization ensure the even distribution of all components within the solution, resulting in a consistent formulation.
- **Steps**:

  - Use mechanical stirrers or homogenizers to mix the solution thoroughly.
  - Adjust the mixing speed and duration based on the viscosity and volume of the solution to achieve uniformity.

4. pH Adjustment

- **Technique**: pH adjustment involves altering the pH of the solution to enhance the solubility and stability of the API.
- **Steps**:

  - Measure the initial pH of the solution.
  - Add appropriate buffering agents or acids/bases to achieve the desired pH.
  - Monitor and adjust the pH as needed throughout the preparation process.

Equipment
1. Weighing Balances

- **Function**: Used for accurately measuring the quantities of API and excipients.
- **Types**: Analytical balances for precise measurements (typically accurate to 0.001 grams).

2. Magnetic Stirrer with Hot Plate

- **Function**: Used for dissolving solutes in solvents with continuous stirring and optional heating.
- **Features**: Variable speed control and temperature settings to optimize dissolution conditions.

3. Mechanical Stirrer

- **Function**: Provides efficient mixing of large volumes of liquid, ensuring uniform distribution of ingredients.
- **Features**: Adjustable speed and different types of stirrer blades (e.g., paddle, impeller) suitable for various viscosities.

4. Homogenizer

- **Function**: Used to achieve a high degree of uniformity and particle size reduction in liquid formulations.
- **Features**: High shear forces generated by the homogenizer improve the mixing and stability of the solution.

5. Filtration Apparatus

- **Function**: Removes particulate matter and impurities from the solution.
- **Types**:

  - **Gravity Filtration**: Simple setup using filter paper and funnel for basic filtration needs.
  - **Vacuum Filtration**: Enhanced filtration efficiency using a vacuum pump to speed up the process.
  - **Membrane Filtration**: High-precision filters (e.g., 0.22-micron filters) for sterile filtration of solutions.

6. pH Meter

- **Function**: Measures the pH of the solution accurately.
- **Features**: Digital readout with calibration capabilities to ensure precise pH adjustments.

7. Glassware

- **Types**:

  - **Volumetric Flasks**: Used for precise measurement and preparation of solutions to specific volumes.
  - **Beakers and Erlenmeyer Flasks**: General-purpose glassware for mixing and dissolving components.
  - **Pipettes and Burettes**: Accurate dispensing and titration of liquids during preparation.

8. Bottles and Containers

- **Function**: Used for storing and packaging the final liquid dosage form.
- **Types**:

  - **Glass Bottles**: Often used for solutions that require protection from light (amber bottles) or when chemical compatibility is a concern.
  - **Plastic Bottles**: Lightweight and shatter-resistant, suitable for various formulations.
  - **Dropper Bottles**: Used for precise dispensing of small volumes, particularly for ophthalmic and nasal solutions.

The preparation of monophasic liquid dosage forms involves a range of techniques and specialized equipment to ensure that the final product is homogeneous, stable, and effective. By employing accurate weighing, efficient dissolution, thorough filtration, and proper mixing, pharmacists can create high-quality liquid formulations. Understanding the role of each piece of equipment and technique is essential for achieving the desired therapeutic outcomes and ensuring patient safety.

Gargles, Mouthwashes, Throat Paint

Definitions and Uses
Gargles:

- **Definition**: Gargles are aqueous solutions used to treat or prevent throat infections. They are meant to be swished around the throat and then expelled, rather than swallowed.

- **Uses**: Gargles are typically used to soothe sore throats, reduce inflammation, and disinfect the mouth and throat area. They may contain antiseptics, anesthetics, antibiotics, or anti-inflammatory agents.

Mouthwashes:

- **Definition**: Mouthwashes are aqueous solutions used for oral hygiene. Unlike gargles, they are swished around the mouth, gums, and teeth, and then spit out. Some therapeutic mouthwashes can be swallowed if they are designed for that purpose.
- **Uses**: Mouthwashes are used to freshen breath, reduce oral bacteria, prevent dental plaque, and treat oral infections. They may contain antiseptics, fluoride, analgesics, or other therapeutic agents.

Throat Paint:

- **Definition**: Throat paint is a viscous liquid formulation applied directly to the mucous membranes of the throat using a brush or applicator. It is more concentrated than gargles and mouthwashes.
- **Uses**: Throat paints are used to provide a prolonged therapeutic effect on the mucous membranes of the throat. They often contain antiseptics, analgesics, or anti-inflammatory agents and are used to treat severe throat infections and inflammation.

Therapeutic Applications and Benefits
Gargles
Therapeutic Applications:

- **Sore Throat Relief**: Gargles are commonly used to provide symptomatic relief for sore throats caused by infections, allergies, or irritants.
- **Antiseptic Action**: Gargles with antiseptic properties help to reduce the bacterial load in the mouth and throat, aiding in the treatment and prevention of infections like pharyngitis and tonsillitis.
- **Anti-inflammatory Effects**: Gargles containing anti-inflammatory agents can help reduce swelling and discomfort in the throat.

Benefits:

- **Local Action**: Gargles act locally at the site of infection or inflammation, providing targeted relief.
- **Ease of Use**: Gargles are simple to use and can be easily incorporated into a daily routine for ongoing throat care.
- **Minimal Systemic Absorption**: Since gargles are not swallowed, there is minimal systemic absorption, reducing the risk of side effects.

Mouthwashes
Therapeutic Applications:

- **Oral Hygiene**: Regular use of mouthwashes helps to maintain oral hygiene by reducing bacteria, preventing plaque formation, and controlling bad breath.
- **Dental Care**: Mouthwashes containing fluoride help to strengthen tooth enamel and prevent dental caries.
- **Treatment of Oral Conditions**: Therapeutic mouthwashes are used to treat conditions such as gingivitis, periodontitis, and oral ulcers.

Benefits:

- **Broad Spectrum**: Mouthwashes can target a wide range of oral health issues, from hygiene maintenance to specific therapeutic needs.
- **Convenience**: Mouthwashes are easy to use and can be quickly integrated into daily oral care routines.
- **Accessibility**: They are widely available over-the-counter, making them accessible for preventive and therapeutic use.

Throat Paint
Therapeutic Applications:

- **Severe Throat Infections**: Throat paints are used to treat severe or persistent throat infections, providing a concentrated dose of medication directly to the affected area.
- **Prolonged Effect**: The viscous nature of throat paint ensures that the medication stays in contact with the mucous membranes for a longer duration, enhancing its therapeutic effect.
- **Pain Relief**: Throat paints often contain analgesics to provide relief from pain associated with throat infections.

Benefits:

- **Targeted Delivery**: Throat paint delivers medication directly to the affected area, ensuring maximum therapeutic efficacy.
- **Long-lasting Relief**: Due to its thicker consistency, throat paint provides longer-lasting relief compared to gargles or mouthwashes.
- **High Potency**: The concentrated nature of throat paints allows for a higher potency of active ingredients, making them effective for severe conditions.

Gargles, mouthwashes, and throat paints each serve distinct purposes in oral and throat care, offering various therapeutic benefits. Gargles are ideal for providing localized relief from throat discomfort and infections, mouthwashes are effective for maintaining oral hygiene and treating a range of oral health conditions, and throat paints are suited for delivering potent, targeted treatment for severe throat infections. Understanding the definitions, uses, therapeutic applications, and benefits of these monophasic liquid dosage forms allows pharmacists and healthcare providers to recommend the most appropriate treatment for patients' specific needs.

Preparation Techniques for Gargles, Mouthwashes, and Throat Paint

Gargles
  Ingredients:

- Active Ingredient: Antiseptic (e.g., povidone-iodine), anesthetic (e.g., benzocaine), or anti-inflammatory agent (e.g., benzydamine hydrochloride)
- Solvent: Purified water
- Flavoring Agents: Peppermint oil or menthol (optional)
- Preservatives: Methylparaben, propylparaben (optional)
- pH Adjusters: Citric acid or sodium hydroxide (optional)

Preparation Steps:

1. **Weighing and Measuring:**

- Accurately weigh the required amounts of active ingredient, preservatives, and flavoring agents.
- Measure the appropriate volume of purified water.

2. **Dissolution**:

- Dissolve the active ingredient in purified water while stirring continuously. Gentle heating may be used if necessary to facilitate dissolution.
- Add preservatives and flavoring agents to the solution and stir until fully dissolved.

3. **pH Adjustment**:

- Adjust the pH of the solution to the desired range (typically 6.0-7.5) using citric acid or sodium hydroxide.

4. **Filtration**:

- Filter the solution through an appropriate filter medium (e.g., filter paper or membrane filter) to remove any particulate matter and ensure clarity.

5. **Mixing**:

- Mix the filtered solution thoroughly to ensure uniform distribution of all components.

6. **Packaging**:

- Fill the solution into clean, sterile bottles and seal with appropriate closures.
- Label the bottles with essential information, including product name, concentration, usage instructions, storage conditions, and expiration date.

Mouthwashes
Ingredients:

- Active Ingredient: Antiseptic (e.g., chlorhexidine gluconate), fluoride (e.g., sodium fluoride), or other therapeutic agents (e.g., hydrogen peroxide)
- Solvent: Purified water, ethanol (optional)
- Sweeteners: Sorbitol, saccharin
- Flavoring Agents: Mint, menthol
- Preservatives: Benzoic acid, sodium benzoate
- pH Adjusters: Citric acid, sodium bicarbonate

Preparation Steps:

1. **Weighing and Measuring:**

   - Accurately weigh the required amounts of active ingredient, sweeteners, flavoring agents, and preservatives.
   - Measure the appropriate volume of purified water and ethanol (if used).

2. **Dissolution:**

   - Dissolve the active ingredient in the solvent(s) while stirring continuously. Gentle heating may be used if necessary.
   - Add sweeteners, flavoring agents, and preservatives to the solution and stir until fully dissolved.

3. **pH Adjustment:**

   - Adjust the pH of the solution to the desired range (typically 5.0-7.0) using citric acid or sodium bicarbonate.

4. **Filtration:**

   - Filter the solution through an appropriate filter medium to remove any particulate matter and ensure clarity.

5. **Mixing:**

- Mix the filtered solution thoroughly to ensure uniform distribution of all components.

6. **Packaging**:

- Fill the solution into clean, sterile bottles and seal with appropriate closures.
- Label the bottles with essential information, including product name, concentration, usage instructions, storage conditions, and expiration date.

Throat Paint
Ingredients:

- Active Ingredient: Antiseptic (e.g., povidone-iodine), analgesic (e.g., phenol), or anti-inflammatory agent
- Solvent: Glycerin, ethanol
- Thickening Agents: Hydroxypropyl methylcellulose (HPMC), xanthan gum
- Flavoring Agents: Mint, menthol
- Preservatives: Methylparaben, propylparaben

Preparation Steps:

1. **Weighing and Measuring**:

- Accurately weigh the required amounts of active ingredient, thickening agents, flavoring agents, and preservatives.
- Measure the appropriate volume of glycerin and ethanol.

2. **Dissolution**:

- Dissolve the active ingredient in glycerin and ethanol while stirring continuously. Gentle heating may be used if necessary.
- Add thickening agents to the solution and stir until a uniform viscosity is achieved.
- Add flavoring agents and preservatives to the solution and stir until fully dissolved.

3. **pH Adjustment**:

- Adjust the pH of the solution to the desired range (typically 5.0-6.5) if necessary.

4. **Filtration**:

- Filter the solution through an appropriate filter medium to remove any particulate matter and ensure clarity.

5. **Mixing and Homogenization**:

- Mix the filtered solution thoroughly to ensure uniform distribution of all components. Homogenization may be required to achieve the desired consistency.

6. **Packaging**:

- Fill the solution into clean, sterile applicator bottles or containers with appropriate closures.
- Label the containers with essential information, including product name, concentration, usage instructions, storage conditions, and expiration date.

The preparation of gargles, mouthwashes, and throat paints involves careful selection of ingredients, precise dissolution, thorough filtration, and appropriate packaging. By following these preparation techniques, pharmacists can ensure that the final product is effective, stable, and safe for patient use. Understanding these methods allows for the consistent production of high-quality monophasic liquid dosage forms tailored to specific therapeutic needs.

Eardrops, Nasal Drops, Enemas

Definitions and Therapeutic Uses
    Eardrops:

- **Definition**: Eardrops are liquid preparations intended for instillation into the ear canal. They typically contain active ingredients such as antibiotics, analgesics, or anti-inflammatory agents.
- **Therapeutic Uses**: Eardrops are used to treat conditions like otitis externa (outer ear infection), otitis media (middle ear infection), ear pain, and cerumen (earwax) impaction.

Nasal Drops

- **Definition**: Nasal drops are liquid preparations intended for instillation into the nasal cavity. They often contain decongestants, antihistamines, or saline solutions.
- **Therapeutic Uses**: Nasal drops are used to relieve nasal congestion, treat allergic rhinitis, reduce inflammation, and moisturize the nasal passages.

Enemas:

- **Definition**: Enemas are liquid preparations introduced into the rectum for cleansing, therapeutic, or diagnostic purposes. They can contain solutions like saline, mineral oil, or medicated substances.
- **Therapeutic Uses**: Enemas are used for bowel cleansing before surgery or diagnostic procedures, treating constipation, delivering medications for local or systemic effects, and reducing inflammation in conditions like ulcerative colitis.

Clinical Applications and Benefits
Eardrops
Clinical Applications:

- **Infections**: Antibiotic eardrops are used to treat bacterial infections of the ear.
- **Pain Relief**: Analgesic eardrops help relieve ear pain associated with infections or injuries.
- **Earwax Removal**: Cerumenolytic agents in eardrops help dissolve earwax, facilitating its removal.

Benefits:

- **Localized Treatment**: Eardrops provide direct delivery of medication to the affected area, enhancing efficacy.
- **Reduced Systemic Side Effects**: Local application minimizes systemic absorption, reducing the risk of side effects.
- **Ease of Use**: Eardrops are easy to administer and can be self-applied.

Nasal Drops
Clinical Applications:

- **Nasal Congestion**: Decongestant nasal drops reduce swelling and congestion in the nasal passages.
- **Allergic Rhinitis**: Antihistamine nasal drops alleviate symptoms of allergies, such as sneezing and runny nose.
- **Nasal Dryness**: Saline nasal drops moisturize and soothe dry nasal passages.

Benefits:

- **Rapid Relief**: Nasal drops provide quick relief from nasal congestion and allergy symptoms.
- **Local Action**: Direct application to the nasal mucosa ensures targeted treatment.
- **Minimal Systemic Effects**: Reduced risk of systemic side effects compared to oral medications.

Enemas
Clinical Applications:

- **Bowel Cleansing**: Enemas are used to cleanse the bowel before surgical or diagnostic procedures.
- **Constipation Relief**: Enemas help relieve constipation by softening stools and stimulating bowel movements.
- **Medication Delivery**: Enemas can deliver medications for local treatment (e.g., anti-inflammatory drugs for ulcerative colitis) or systemic absorption.

Benefits:

- **Effective Cleansing**: Enemas provide thorough bowel cleansing, essential for certain medical procedures.
- **Rapid Action**: They offer quick relief from constipation and other bowel-related issues.
- **Targeted Therapy**: Enemas allow direct delivery of medications to the rectal area, enhancing their therapeutic effect.

Formulation and Preparation

Eardrops

Ingredients:

- Active Ingredient: Antibiotics (e.g., ciprofloxacin), analgesics (e.g., lidocaine), anti-inflammatory agents (e.g., hydrocortisone)
- Solvent: Purified water, propylene glycol, glycerin
- Preservatives: Benzalkonium chloride, phenylmercuric nitrate
- pH Adjusters: Sodium hydroxide, hydrochloric acid

Preparation Steps:

1. **Dissolution**: Dissolve the active ingredient in the solvent with continuous stirring. Gentle heating may be used if necessary.
2. **Addition of Preservatives**: Add preservatives to the solution and ensure they are fully dissolved.
3. **pH Adjustment**: Adjust the pH to the desired range (typically 5.0-7.0) using pH adjusters.
4. **Filtration**: Filter the solution through an appropriate filter to remove particulate matter.
5. **Packaging**: Fill the solution into sterile dropper bottles and seal with appropriate closures. Label with usage instructions and expiration date.

Nasal Drops

Ingredients:

- Active Ingredient: Decongestants (e.g., oxymetazoline), antihistamines (e.g., azelastine), saline
- Solvent: Purified water
- Preservatives: Benzalkonium chloride, phenylmercuric nitrate
- pH Adjusters: Sodium hydroxide, hydrochloric acid

Preparation Steps:

1. **Dissolution**: Dissolve the active ingredient in purified water with continuous stirring.
2. **Addition of Preservatives**: Add preservatives and ensure they are fully dissolved.
3. **pH Adjustment**: Adjust the pH to the desired range (typically 5.5-6.5) using pH adjusters.
4. **Filtration**: Filter the solution through an appropriate filter to ensure clarity and sterility.
5. **Packaging**: Fill the solution into sterile nasal dropper bottles and seal with appropriate closures. Label with usage instructions and expiration date.

Enemas
Ingredients:

- Active Ingredient: Laxatives (e.g., sodium phosphate), anti-inflammatory agents (e.g., hydrocortisone), isotonic solutions (e.g., saline)
- Solvent: Purified water
- Preservatives: Benzalkonium chloride (optional)

Preparation Steps:

1. **Dissolution**: Dissolve the active ingredient in purified water with continuous stirring.
2. **Addition of Preservatives**: Add preservatives if necessary and ensure they are fully dissolved.
3. **Filtration**: Filter the solution to remove particulate matter and ensure clarity.
4. **Sterilization**: Sterilize the solution using an appropriate method (e.g., autoclaving, filtration).
5. **Packaging**: Fill the solution into sterile enema containers or bags and seal with appropriate closures. Label with usage instructions and expiration date.

Specific Examples and Case Studies

Example 1: Eardrops for Otitis Externa

- **Formulation**: Ciprofloxacin (0.3%), Hydrocortisone (1%), Propylene Glycol, Benzalkonium Chloride
- **Preparation**: Dissolve ciprofloxacin and hydrocortisone in propylene glycol with continuous stirring. Add benzalkonium chloride as a preservative. Adjust the pH to 6.5. Filter and package in sterile dropper bottles.
- **Case Study**: A patient with otitis externa experienced significant relief from pain and infection after using the formulated eardrops twice daily for one week.

Example 2: Nasal Drops for Allergic Rhinitis

- **Formulation**: Azelastine (0.1%), Sodium Chloride, Purified Water, Benzalkonium Chloride
- **Preparation**: Dissolve azelastine and sodium chloride in purified water. Add benzalkonium chloride as a preservative. Adjust the pH to 6.0. Filter and package in sterile nasal dropper bottles.
- **Case Study**: A patient with allergic rhinitis reported reduced nasal congestion and sneezing after using the nasal drops twice daily for one week.

Example 3: Enema for Bowel Cleansing

- **Formulation**. Sodium Phosphate (19 g), Purified Water (1000 mL)
- **Preparation**: Dissolve sodium phosphate in purified water with continuous stirring. Filter the solution to remove particulate matter. Sterilize by autoclaving. Package in sterile enema bags.
- **Case Study**: A patient scheduled for a colonoscopy used the enema as instructed, resulting in effective bowel cleansing and successful completion of the diagnostic procedure.

CHAPTER NINE

Biphasic Liquids

Introduction to Biphasic Liquids

Biphasic liquids are a unique and versatile category of pharmaceutical dosage forms that consist of two distinct phases: a dispersed phase and a continuous phase. These systems are designed to deliver therapeutic agents efficiently by leveraging the physical and chemical properties of both phases to optimize drug stability, bioavailability, and patient compliance. Biphasic liquids are commonly employed in various medical applications, ranging from oral and topical to injectable formulations.

Definition and Characteristics

Biphasic liquids, also known as biphasic systems or biphasic dosage forms, are heterogeneous mixtures where one phase (the dispersed phase) is finely distributed within another phase (the continuous phase). The two phases can be in different physical states, such as solid-in-liquid (suspensions) or liquid-in-liquid (emulsions), and are typically immiscible. This immiscibility is a defining characteristic that requires careful formulation to ensure stability and uniformity.

Types of Biphasic Liquids

1. **Suspensions:**

   ○ **Definition:** A suspension is a biphasic liquid dosage form in which fine particles of a solid drug are dispersed throughout a liquid medium in which the drug is not soluble. The solid particles remain suspended in the liquid phase, creating a heterogeneous system that must be shaken before use to ensure uniform distribution.

- **Components:**

  - **Dispersed Phase (Solid):** The finely divided solid drug particles.
  - **Dispersion Medium (Liquid):** The liquid in which the solid particles are dispersed, such as water or oil.
  - **Suspending Agents:** Substances added to increase the viscosity of the liquid medium and prevent the solid particles from settling too quickly.

2. **Emulsions:**

   - **Definition:** An emulsion is a biphasic liquid dosage form consisting of two immiscible liquids, where one liquid (the dispersed phase) is finely dispersed within the other (the continuous phase). Emulsions are stabilized by emulsifying agents to prevent the two phases from separating.
   - **Components:**

     - **Dispersed Phase (Internal Phase):** The liquid that is dispersed in the form of droplets.
     - **Continuous Phase (External Phase):** The liquid in which the droplets are dispersed.
     - **Emulsifying Agents:** Substances that stabilize the emulsion by reducing the surface tension between the two immiscible liquids.

Importance and Benefits

Biphasic liquids play a crucial role in pharmaceutical formulations due to their ability to enhance drug stability, improve bioavailability, and facilitate patient compliance. The key benefits of biphasic liquids include:

1. **Enhanced Stability:**

   - **Chemical Stability:** Biphasic liquids can protect drugs from degradation by isolating them in a separate phase, thus minimizing exposure to factors that cause hydrolysis or oxidation.

- ◦ **Microbial Stability:** Proper formulation with preservatives can reduce the risk of microbial contamination.

2. **Improved Bioavailability:**

   - ◦ **Rapid Absorption:** The fine particles or droplets in biphasic liquids can enhance the dissolution rate of drugs, leading to quicker absorption and onset of action.
   - ◦ **Dose Flexibility:** Biphasic liquids allow for easy dose adjustment, particularly beneficial for pediatric and geriatric patients.

3. **Patient Compliance:**

   - ◦ **Ease of Administration:** Biphasic liquids are often easier to swallow than solid dosage forms, making them suitable for patients who have difficulty swallowing tablets or capsules.
   - ◦ **Taste Masking:** Unpleasant tastes can be masked more effectively in biphasic formulations, improving patient adherence to the medication regimen.

Challenges and Considerations

Despite their advantages, biphasic liquids also present certain challenges that must be addressed during formulation:

1. **Physical Instability:**

   - ◦ **Sedimentation and Caking:** In suspensions, solid particles tend to settle over time, which can lead to non-uniform distribution and difficulty in redispersing if caking occurs.
   - ◦ **Phase Separation:** In emulsions, the dispersed droplets may coalesce, leading to phase separation if not properly stabilized.

2. **Dosage Uniformity:**

   - ◦ **Inconsistent Dosing:** Ensuring a uniform dose can be challenging, especially if the biphasic liquid is not adequately shaken before use.
   - ◦ **Accuracy of Measurement:** Patients must use appropriate measuring devices to ensure accurate dosing.

3. **Formulation Complexity:**

   - **Selection of Excipients:** Formulating a stable biphasic liquid requires careful selection of suspending agents, emulsifying agents, preservatives, and other excipients.
   - **Storage and Handling:** Biphasic liquids may require specific storage conditions to maintain stability, such as protection from freezing or excessive heat.

Practical Applications

Biphasic liquids are widely used in various therapeutic areas, including:

1. **Oral Suspensions:** Commonly used for pediatric formulations, such as antibiotic suspensions (e.g., amoxicillin) and antacid suspensions (e.g., magnesium hydroxide).
2. **Topical Emulsions:** Used for dermatological applications, such as corticosteroid creams (e.g., hydrocortisone) and moisturizing lotions.
3. **Injectable Emulsions:** Employed for intravenous administration, such as lipid emulsions for parenteral nutrition and certain chemotherapeutic agents.

Biphasic liquids are a vital category of pharmaceutical dosage forms that offer significant benefits in terms of stability, bioavailability, and patient compliance. Understanding the characteristics, advantages, and challenges of biphasic liquids is essential for pharmacists and healthcare providers to optimize their use and ensure effective and safe medication delivery. By leveraging the unique properties of biphasic systems, it is possible to develop formulations that meet diverse therapeutic needs and improve patient outcomes.

Classification and Preparation of Suspensions

Suspensions are versatile dosage forms in pharmaceuticals, classified based on particle size, nature of the dispersed phase, and sedimentation behavior. Understanding these classifications is crucial for selecting the appropriate formulation and preparation techniques for specific therapeutic needs.

Types of Suspensions

1. **Based on Particle Size:**

   - **Coarse Suspensions:** Contain large particles, usually greater than 1 micron in diameter. These are more prone to sedimentation.
   - **Colloidal Suspensions:** Contain very fine particles, typically less than 1 micron, which remain dispersed for a longer time and exhibit better stability.

2. **Based on Nature of Dispersed Phase:**

   - **Oral Suspensions:** Designed for oral administration, often containing flavoring agents and sweeteners to improve palatability.
   - **Topical Suspensions:** Intended for skin application, formulated to ensure adherence and provide sustained release of the active ingredient.
   - **Ophthalmic Suspensions:** Sterile suspensions for eye instillation, formulated to avoid irritation and ensure sterility.
   - **Parenteral Suspensions:** Sterile suspensions for injection, requiring stringent controls to ensure sterility and avoid particle aggregation.

3. **Based on Sedimentation Behavior:**

   - **Flocculated Suspensions:** Particles form loose aggregates (flocs) which settle rapidly but are easily re-dispersed with gentle shaking.
   - **Deflocculated Suspensions:** Particles remain as separate entities and settle slowly, forming a dense sediment that may be difficult to re-disperse.

Step-by-Step Preparation Process

The preparation of suspensions involves several critical steps to ensure uniformity, stability, and efficacy.

Step 1: Selection of Ingredients

- **Active Pharmaceutical Ingredient (API):** Select based on therapeutic use.
- **Vehicle:** Choose a suitable liquid medium (e.g., water, oil).

- **Suspending Agents:** Add agents like methylcellulose, carboxymethylcellulose, or xanthan gum to increase viscosity and prevent sedimentation.
- **Preservatives:** Include preservatives such as parabens or benzalkonium chloride to prevent microbial growth.
- **Flocculating Agents:** Use agents like electrolytes if a flocculated suspension is desired.
- **Other Excipients:** Add sweeteners, flavoring agents, and coloring agents as needed.

Step 2: Preparation of the Dispersed Phase

- **Micronization:** Reduce the particle size of the API using techniques such as milling or grinding to achieve the desired fineness.

Step 3: Wetting of Particles

- **Wetting Agents:** Use surfactants like polysorbates to wet the hydrophobic particles, ensuring even dispersion in the liquid medium.

Step 4: Mixing and Dispersion

- **Mixing Equipment:** Use mechanical stirrers or homogenizers to disperse the API in the vehicle, ensuring thorough mixing for a uniform suspension.

Step 5: Addition of Suspending Agents

- **Dissolution:** Dissolve the suspending agents in a portion of the vehicle, then add this solution to the dispersion to increase viscosity.

Step 6: pH Adjustment

- **pH Adjusters:** Adjust the pH of the suspension to optimize stability and solubility of the API.

Step 7: Homogenization

- **Homogenization Equipment:** Pass the suspension through a homogenizer to ensure uniform particle size distribution and prevent aggregation.

Step 8: Filtration and Sterilization (if required)

- **Filtration:** Filter the suspension to remove any large particles or contaminants.
- **Sterilization:** Use appropriate sterilization techniques (e.g., autoclaving, sterile filtration) for ophthalmic and parenteral suspensions.

Step 9: Packaging

- **Filling Equipment:** Fill the suspension into suitable containers under aseptic conditions if required. Use containers that protect the suspension from light and air.
- **Labeling:** Label containers with essential information, including product name, concentration, usage instructions, storage conditions, and expiration date.

Practical Examples and Recipes

Example 1: Oral Antacid Suspension
Ingredients:

- Magnesium Hydroxide: 400 mg
- Aluminum Hydroxide: 400 mg
- Simethicone: 40 mg
- Methylcellulose: 1 g
- Saccharin Sodium: 0.1 g
- Peppermint Oil: 0.05 g
- Purified Water: qs to 100 mL

Preparation:

1. **Micronization:** Micronize the magnesium hydroxide and aluminum hydroxide to reduce particle size.

2. **Wetting:** Use polysorbate 80 to wet the particles.
3. **Suspending Agent Solution:** Dissolve methylcellulose in a portion of purified water.
4. **Dispersion:** Disperse the wet particles in the vehicle with continuous stirring.
5. **Addition of Simethicone and Sweeteners:** Add simethicone, saccharin sodium, and peppermint oil to the dispersion.
6. **Mixing:** Thoroughly mix and homogenize the suspension.
7. **Packaging:** Fill into amber bottles and label appropriately.

Example 2: Topical Corticosteroid Suspension
Ingredients:

- Hydrocortisone: 1 g
- Propylene Glycol: 10 mL
- Xanthan Gum: 0.5 g
- Glycerin: 5 mL
- Methylparaben: 0.1 g
- Purified Water: qs to 100 mL

Preparation:

1. **Micronization:** Micronize the hydrocortisone.
2. **Wetting:** Wet the hydrocortisone with propylene glycol.
3. **Suspending Agent Solution:** Dissolve xanthan gum and glycerin in purified water.
4. **Dispersion:** Disperse the wetted hydrocortisone in the suspending agent solution with continuous stirring.
5. **Addition of Preservative:** Add methylparaben and stir until fully dissolved.
6. **Homogenization:** Pass the suspension through a homogenizer to ensure uniform particle size distribution.
7. **Packaging:** Fill into suitable applicator bottles and label appropriately.

Example 3: Ophthalmic Antibiotic Suspension
Ingredients:

- Ciprofloxacin: 0.3 g

- Benzalkonium Chloride: 0.01 g
- Hydroxypropyl Methylcellulose: 0.5 g
- Sodium Chloride: 0.9 g
- Purified Water: qs to 100 mL

Preparation:

1. **Micronization:** Micronize the ciprofloxacin.
2. **Wetting:** Wet the ciprofloxacin with a suitable wetting agent.
3. **Suspending Agent Solution:** Dissolve hydroxypropyl methylcellulose and sodium chloride in purified water.
4. **Dispersion:** Disperse the wetted ciprofloxacin in the suspending agent solution with continuous stirring.
5. **Addition of Preservative:** Add benzalkonium chloride and stir until fully dissolved.
6. **Sterilization:** Sterilize the suspension by autoclaving.
7. **Filtration:** Filter the sterilized suspension through a 0.22-micron filter to ensure sterility.
8. **Packaging:** Fill into sterile dropper bottles under aseptic conditions and label appropriately.

Flocculated vs. Deflocculated Suspensions: Definitions and Differences

Flocculated Suspensions

Definition: Flocculated suspensions contain particles that are loosely bonded together to form light, fluffy aggregates called flocs. These flocs settle rapidly but can be easily redispersed with gentle shaking.

Differences:

- Particles are held together in loose networks by weak bonds, such as van der Waals forces.
- This allows them to settle quickly but also be easily broken apart and resuspended.

Deflocculated Suspensions

Definition: Deflocculated suspensions contain individual particles that remain separate from each other. These particles settle slowly and form a dense sediment that can be difficult to redisperse.

Differences:

- Particles are individually dispersed and remain separated by electrostatic repulsion or steric hindrance.
- This leads to slower sedimentation but more difficult redispersion.

Key Characteristics of Each Type
Flocculated Suspensions
Sedimentation:

- Particles form loose aggregates (flocs) that settle rapidly.

Redispersion:

- Easy to redisperse upon shaking, as the flocs break apart readily.

Appearance:

- Often cloudy due to the presence of flocs.

Viscosity:

- Generally lower viscosity compared to deflocculated suspensions, as the flocs do not contribute much to the overall viscosity of the suspension.

Deflocculated Suspensions
Sedimentation:

- Particles settle slowly and form a compact, dense sediment.

Redispersion:

- Difficult to redisperse once settled, as the particles form a hard cake.

Appearance:

- Typically clearer than flocculated suspensions when undisturbed.

Viscosity:

- Higher viscosity due to the individual particles contributing to the resistance to flow.

Characteristics and Selection Criteria
Flocculated Suspensions
Ease of Use:

- Preferred when ease of redispersion is important, ensuring consistent dosing with each administration.

Application:

- Suitable for products that are frequently used and need to be easily redispersed, such as oral suspensions for pediatric use.

Deflocculated Suspensions
Stability:

- Preferred when a slower sedimentation rate is desired to maintain a uniform suspension for a longer period.

Application:

- Suitable for products where long-term storage stability is crucial, such as certain injectable suspensions.

Criteria for Choosing the Appropriate Type
Intended Use:

- Consider the frequency of use and the need for ease of redispersion. For frequent use, flocculated suspensions are ideal.

Storage Conditions:

- Evaluate the expected storage conditions and duration. Deflocculated suspensions may be more stable for long-term storage.

Viscosity Requirements:

- Determine the desired viscosity of the final product. Higher viscosity may be achieved with deflocculated suspensions.

Patient Compliance:

- For patient-friendly formulations, especially for children or the elderly, flocculated suspensions are often preferred due to easier redispersion.

Comparative Stability and Efficacy
Stability:
Flocculated Suspensions:

- The rapid sedimentation and ease of redispersion make flocculated suspensions stable in terms of maintaining uniform dosing.
- However, the rapid settling can be a disadvantage if the suspension is not frequently used and shaken.

Deflocculated Suspensions:

- The slower sedimentation rate can enhance the stability of the suspension over time, maintaining a uniform appearance for a longer duration.
- However, the formation of a hard cake upon settling can pose a significant challenge for redispersion.

Efficacy:
Flocculated Suspensions:

- Ensuring consistent therapeutic efficacy with each dose, as the suspension can be easily redispersed to achieve a uniform concentration of the active ingredient.

Deflocculated Suspensions:

- Potentially better for maintaining a uniform suspension during storage, but the difficulty in redispersing the sediment can lead to variability in dosing and reduced therapeutic efficacy.

Analysis of Stability and Therapeutic Effectiveness
Stability Analysis:
Flocculated Suspensions:

- Stability can be assessed by observing the rate of sedimentation and the ease of redispersion.
- Frequent agitation or shaking is essential to maintain homogeneity.

Deflocculated Suspensions:

- Stability is assessed by monitoring the rate of sedimentation and the hardness of the sediment formed.
- Minimizing the formation of a hard cake is crucial for maintaining stability.

Therapeutic Effectiveness:
Flocculated Suspensions:

- Therapeutic effectiveness is maintained through easy redispersion, ensuring a consistent dose with each administration.
- This is particularly important for suspensions that require precise dosing.

Deflocculated Suspensions:

- Therapeutic effectiveness can be compromised if the suspension is not adequately redispersed before administration.

Flocculated and deflocculated suspensions each have unique characteristics, advantages, and limitations. Flocculated suspensions offer ease of redispersion and consistent dosing, making them ideal for frequent use and patient-friendly formulations. Deflocculated suspensions provide slower sedimentation and potentially better long-term stability but can pose challenges with redispersion. By understanding these differences and considering the specific needs of the formulation and patient population, pharmacists can select the appropriate type of suspension to ensure optimal stability and therapeutic efficacy.

The comprehensive understanding of flocculated and deflocculated suspensions, their preparation, stability, and therapeutic effectiveness allows for better pharmaceutical formulations tailored to meet patient needs and improve compliance.

Stability Problems and Solutions in Suspensions

Suspensions are prone to various stability problems due to the nature of their biphasic system. These issues can affect the physical, chemical, and microbiological stability of the suspension. Addressing these problems is essential to ensure the efficacy, safety, and patient compliance of the medication.

Common Stability Issues

1. **Sedimentation:**

   - **Issue:** Particles in a suspension tend to settle over time due to gravity, leading to non-uniform distribution of the active ingredient.
   - **Problem:** This can result in inconsistent dosing and reduced therapeutic efficacy.

2. **Caking:**

   - **Issue:** Once the particles settle, they may form a dense, compact sediment that is difficult to redisperse.
   - **Problem:** Caking makes it challenging to achieve a uniform suspension after shaking, leading to dosing inaccuracies.

3. **Flocculation:**

   - **Issue:** Particles aggregate loosely, forming flocs that settle rapidly.
   - **Problem:** While flocs are easier to redisperse, rapid sedimentation can still lead to dosing issues if not adequately addressed.

4. **Particle Size Growth (Ostwald Ripening):**

   - **Issue:** Smaller particles dissolve and redeposit onto larger particles, leading to an increase in particle size over time.

- ○ **Problem:** This can affect the suspension's stability and the rate of dissolution of the active ingredient.

5. **Chemical Degradation:**

   - ○ **Issue:** The active ingredient or excipients may degrade over time due to hydrolysis, oxidation, or other chemical reactions.
   - ○ **Problem:** Chemical degradation reduces the potency and efficacy of the suspension.

6. **Microbial Contamination:**

   - ○ **Issue:** Suspensions are susceptible to microbial growth due to the presence of water and nutrients.
   - ○ **Problem:** Microbial contamination can spoil the product and pose health risks to patients.

Techniques to Improve Stability

Several techniques can be employed to enhance the stability of suspensions, addressing the common issues mentioned above.

1. **Use of Suspending Agents:**

   - ○ **Function:** Increase the viscosity of the suspension medium, reducing the rate of sedimentation.
   - ○ **Examples:** Methylcellulose, carboxymethylcellulose, xanthan gum.
   - ○ **Application:** Carefully select and optimize the concentration of suspending agents to balance viscosity and ease of redispersion.

2. **Flocculating Agents:**

   - ○ **Function:** Induce the formation of loose aggregates (flocs) that settle rapidly but are easy to redisperse.
   - ○ **Examples:** Electrolytes (e.g., sodium chloride), polymers (e.g., gelatin).
   - ○ **Application:** Adjust the concentration of flocculating agents to achieve the desired balance between sedimentation rate and ease of redispersion.

3. **Particle Size Reduction:**

- **Function:** Smaller particles settle more slowly and form a more uniform suspension.
- **Methods:** Milling, micronization.
- **Application:** Optimize the particle size of the active ingredient during formulation.

4. **Use of Wetting Agents:**

- **Function:** Enhance the dispersibility of hydrophobic particles in the suspension medium.
- **Examples:** Surfactants such as polysorbates (Tween 80), sodium lauryl sulfate.
- **Application:** Select appropriate wetting agents to ensure uniform dispersion of particles.

5. **pH Adjustment:**

- **Function:** Optimize the pH to enhance the chemical stability of the active ingredient and excipients.
- **Application:** Use buffering agents to maintain the desired pH range.

6. **Preservatives:**

- **Function:** Prevent microbial growth and contamination.
- **Examples:** Parabens (methylparaben, propylparaben), benzalkonium chloride.
- **Application:** Include preservatives in the formulation and ensure they are compatible with other ingredients.

7. **Antioxidants:**

- **Function:** Prevent oxidation of the active ingredient and excipients.
- **Examples:** Ascorbic acid, sodium metabisulfite.
- **Application:** Add antioxidants to protect the formulation from oxidative degradation.

Case Studies and Practical Solutions

Case Study 1: Improving the Stability of an Oral Antibiotic Suspension

Problem: An oral antibiotic suspension exhibited rapid sedimentation and caking, making it difficult to redisperse.

Solution:

- **Suspending Agents:** Added methylcellulose to increase the viscosity and reduce sedimentation.
- **Flocculating Agents:** Added sodium citrate to induce flocculation, ensuring the particles settled as loose aggregates.
- **Wetting Agents:** Used polysorbate 80 to enhance the dispersibility of the antibiotic particles.

Outcome: The modified formulation showed significantly improved stability, with easy redispersion and consistent dosing.

Case Study 2: Addressing Chemical Degradation in a Topical Corticosteroid Suspension

Problem: A topical corticosteroid suspension exhibited chemical degradation of the active ingredient, reducing its efficacy.

Solution:

- **pH Adjustment:** Adjusted the pH to the optimal range for the stability of the corticosteroid using a phosphate buffer.
- **Antioxidants:** Added ascorbic acid to prevent oxidative degradation.

Outcome: The reformulated suspension demonstrated enhanced chemical stability, maintaining the potency of the corticosteroid over its shelf life.

Case Study 3: Preventing Microbial Contamination in an Ophthalmic Suspension

Problem: An ophthalmic suspension was prone to microbial contamination, posing a risk to patients.

Solution:

- **Preservatives:** Included benzalkonium chloride as a preservative to inhibit microbial growth.
- **Sterilization:** Sterilized the final product using autoclaving and aseptic filling techniques.

Outcome: The inclusion of preservatives and proper sterilization ensured the microbial stability of the ophthalmic suspension, making it safe for patient use.

Additional Stability Improvement Techniques

Use of Controlled Release Formulations:

- **Function:** Modify the release of the active ingredient to enhance stability and therapeutic efficacy.
- **Example:** Microencapsulation techniques to protect the active ingredient from degradation and control the release rate.

Optimization of Storage Conditions:

- **Function:** Store suspensions under conditions that minimize degradation and maintain stability.
- **Example:** Refrigeration or storage in dark, cool environments to protect the suspension from light and heat.

Advanced Analytical Techniques:

- **Function:** Utilize sophisticated analytical methods to monitor and ensure the stability of suspensions over time.
- **Example:** High-performance liquid chromatography (HPLC) and particle size analysis to assess chemical and physical stability.

Stability issues in suspensions can significantly impact their efficacy and patient compliance. By understanding common stability problems and employing appropriate techniques, such as the use of suspending agents, flocculating agents, particle size reduction, wetting agents, pH adjustment, preservatives, and antioxidants, pharmacists can enhance the stability and effectiveness of suspension formulations. Real-world case studies illustrate the practical application of these solutions, demonstrating how thoughtful formulation adjustments can address specific stability challenges and improve therapeutic outcomes.

Emulsions in Pharmaceutical Forms: Definition, Classification, and Emulsifying Agents

Basic Definition

Emulsions: Emulsions are biphasic liquid dosage forms consisting of two immiscible liquids, where one liquid (the dispersed phase) is finely dispersed in the other (the continuous phase) with the help of emulsifying agents. This results in a heterogeneous system where tiny droplets of one liquid are dispersed throughout another.

Key Components:

- **Dispersed Phase:** The liquid dispersed in the form of small droplets.
- **Continuous Phase:** The liquid in which the dispersed phase is distributed.
- **Emulsifying Agents:** Surfactants or stabilizers that reduce interfacial tension between the two immiscible liquids and stabilize the droplets.

Understanding Emulsions in Pharmaceutical Forms

Emulsions are vital in pharmaceutical formulations for delivering drugs that are insoluble or poorly soluble in water. They are used in various administration routes, including oral, topical, and parenteral, to enhance the bioavailability of hydrophobic drugs, improve patient compliance, and allow for controlled release of active ingredients.

Key Characteristics:

- **Appearance:** Milky or opaque liquids due to light scattering by dispersed droplets.
- **Texture:** Can vary from liquid to semi-solid, depending on the formulation.
- **Stability:** Requires proper formulation to prevent phase separation, coalescence of droplets, and creaming.

Types of Emulsions

Emulsions are classified based on phase distribution and the nature of the dispersed and continuous phases.

Classification Based on Phase Distribution:

1. Oil-in-Water (O/W) Emulsions:

   - **Definition:** Oil droplets dispersed in an aqueous continuous phase.
   - **Characteristics:** Milky or creamy appearance, used for oral and topical formulations.

- ◦ **Advantages:** Easier to wash off, comfortable for patients, better absorption through the skin when used topically.

2. Water-in-Oil (W/O) Emulsions:

- ◦ **Definition:** Water droplets dispersed in an oily continuous phase.
- ◦ **Characteristics:** Greasier and thicker than O/W emulsions, used for topical formulations.
- ◦ **Advantages:** Provides an occlusive barrier, improving skin hydration and protection.

3. Multiple Emulsions:

- ◦ **Definition:** Complex systems where an O/W emulsion is further dispersed in oil (O/W/O) or a W/O emulsion is further dispersed in water (W/O/W).
- ◦ **Characteristics:** Comprise two emulsions, allowing for controlled release and targeted delivery of active ingredients.
- ◦ **Advantages:** Encapsulate both hydrophilic and lipophilic drugs, providing dual release profiles.

Detailed Classification:

1. Simple Emulsions:

- ◦ **O/W Emulsions:**

  - ▪ **Continuous Phase:** Water
  - ▪ **Dispersed Phase:** Oil
  - ▪ **Examples:** Milk, aqueous creams, oral liquid emulsions.

- ◦ **W/O Emulsions:**

  - ▪ **Continuous Phase:** Oil
  - ▪ **Dispersed Phase:** Water
  - ▪ **Examples:** Cold creams, moisturizing ointments.

2. Complex Emulsions:

- ◦ **Multiple Emulsions:**

  - ▪ **O/W/O Emulsions:**

    - ▪ **Inner Phase:** Oil
    - ▪ **Middle Phase:** Water
    - ▪ **Outer Phase:** Oil
    - ▪ **Example:** Used in cosmetics for sustained release of active ingredients.

  - ▪ **W/O/W Emulsions:**

    - ▪ **Inner Phase:** Water
    - ▪ **Middle Phase:** Oil
    - ▪ **Outer Phase:** Water
    - ▪ **Example:** Used in pharmaceuticals for encapsulating and delivering both hydrophilic and hydrophobic drugs.

Emulsifying Agents
Role and Importance
Role of Emulsifying Agents:

- **Stabilization:** Reduce the interfacial tension between immiscible phases (oil and water), preventing coalescence of dispersed droplets.
- **Formation:** Facilitate the dispersion of one liquid phase into another, creating and maintaining small droplet sizes.
- **Consistency:** Contribute to the emulsion's texture and palatability, making it acceptable for various administration routes.

Importance in Formulations:

- **Enhanced Stability:** Prevent phase separation, ensuring stability and homogeneity over the shelf life.
- **Improved Bioavailability:** Enhance the bioavailability of hydrophobic drugs by forming stable emulsions.
- **Patient Compliance:** Improve sensory attributes (taste, texture, appearance), enhancing patient compliance.

Types of Emulsifying Agents

1. **Natural Emulsifying Agents:**

   - **Examples:** Acacia (gum arabic), tragacanth, gelatin, lecithin.
   - **Properties:** Biocompatible, biodegradable, generally safe, but susceptible to microbial contamination.

2. **Synthetic Emulsifying Agents:**

   - **Examples:** Polysorbates (Tween 20, Tween 80), sorbitan esters (Span 20, Span 80), polyoxyethylene stearates.
   - **Properties:** Consistent quality, effective at lower concentrations, resistant to microbial contamination, but may cause irritation in sensitive individuals.

3. **Semi-Synthetic Emulsifying Agents:**

   - **Examples:** Methylcellulose, carboxymethylcellulose, hydroxypropyl methylcellulose.
   - **Properties:** Improved stability and functionality compared to natural emulsifiers, with better control over properties through chemical modification.

4. **Finely Divided Solids:**

   - **Examples:** Bentonite, magnesium hydroxide, aluminum hydroxide.
   - **Properties:** Form a physical barrier at the oil-water interface, stabilizing the emulsion through steric mechanisms.

5. **Amphiphilic Polymers:**

   - **Examples:** Polyvinyl alcohol, carbomers, polyacrylamides.
   - **Properties:** Stabilize emulsions through both steric and electrostatic mechanisms, providing excellent stability.

Selection Criteria
Factors Influencing the Choice of Emulsifiers:

1. **Nature of the Emulsion:**

   - **O/W vs. W/O:** The type of emulsion influences the choice of emulsifier. Hydrophilic emulsifiers (e.g., polysorbates) are suitable for O/W emulsions, while lipophilic emulsifiers (e.g., sorbitan esters) are preferred for W/O emulsions.

2. **Hydrophilic-Lipophilic Balance (HLB):**

   - **Definition:** The HLB value measures the balance between the hydrophilic and lipophilic parts of an emulsifier. Emulsifiers with an HLB value of 8-18 are suitable for O/W emulsions, while those with an HLB value of 3-6 are ideal for W/O emulsions.

3. **Compatibility:**

   - **Physicochemical Compatibility:** The emulsifier must be compatible with active pharmaceutical ingredients (APIs) and other excipients to avoid undesirable interactions.
   - **Formulation pH:** The stability and effectiveness of emulsifiers can be pH-dependent. Consider the final formulation's pH when selecting an emulsifier.

4. **Regulatory and Safety Considerations:**

   - **Toxicity and Irritation:** The chosen emulsifier should be non-toxic and non-irritating for the intended administration route. Regulatory approval and safety data must ensure compliance with health regulations.

5. **Desired Characteristics of the Final Product:**

   - **Viscosity and Texture:** The emulsifier should contribute to the desired viscosity and texture, whether a thick cream, fluid lotion, or stable injectable suspension.
   - **Shelf Life and Stability:** Emulsifiers should enhance shelf life and stability, preventing phase separation, creaming, and microbial growth over the intended storage period.

Practical Examples
Example 1: O/W Emulsion for Oral Administration

- **Formulation:** Vitamin E oil (dispersed phase), water (continuous phase), Tween 80 (emulsifying agent).
- **HLB Value:** Tween 80 has an HLB value of 15, suitable for stabilizing oil-in-water emulsions.
- **Characteristics:** The emulsion is stable, with a pleasant mouthfeel and improved bioavailability of the lipophilic vitamin.

Example 2: W/O Emulsion for Topical Use

- **Formulation:** Water (dispersed phase), mineral oil (continuous phase), Span 80 (emulsifying agent).
- **HLB Value:** Span 80 has an HLB value of 4.3, ideal for stabilizing water-in-oil emulsions.
- **Characteristics:** The emulsion provides a moisturizing effect with a protective barrier, suitable for dry skin conditions.

Example 3: Injectable Emulsion

- **Formulation:** Soybean oil (dispersed phase), water (continuous phase), lecithin (natural emulsifying agent), polysorbate 80 (synthetic emulsifying agent).
- **Selection Criteria:** Lecithin and polysorbate 80 are chosen for their biocompatibility and ability to stabilize the emulsion, ensuring safe and effective intravenous administration.

Emulsifying agents play a critical role in forming and stabilizing pharmaceutical emulsions. The choice of emulsifier depends on the type of emulsion, desired properties, and specific formulation requirements. By understanding the role, types, and selection criteria for emulsifying agents, pharmacists and formulators can create stable, effective, and patient-friendly emulsions for various therapeutic applications. This comprehensive understanding ensures that emulsions are formulated to meet patient needs, enhance drug delivery, and improve therapeutic outcomes.

Tests for Identification of Emulsion Types

Emulsions are biphasic liquid systems consisting of two immiscible liquids, with one dispersed as small droplets within the other. Identifying the type of emulsion—whether oil-in-water (O/W) or water-in-oil (W/O)—is crucial for ensuring proper formulation, stability, and application. Several tests can help identify emulsion types, providing valuable information about their characteristics and stability. Here is an extensive look at these tests:

1. Dilution Test:

Principle: The dilution test is based on the solubility of the continuous phase. This test helps to identify whether the emulsion is oil-in-water (O/W) or water-in-oil (W/O) by observing how it reacts when more of the potential continuous phase is added.

Procedure:

- **Step 1:** Take a small sample of the emulsion to be tested.
- **Step 2:** Gradually add a small amount of water to the emulsion.
- **Step 3:** Stir the mixture gently to ensure even distribution of the added water.
- **Step 4:** Observe the emulsion for any signs of instability or separation over a short period (usually a few minutes).

Interpretation:

- **Oil-in-Water (O/W) Emulsion:** If the emulsion remains stable upon the addition of water, it indicates that the continuous phase is water. The added water mixes well with the continuous phase, maintaining the emulsion's stability. The droplets of oil remain dispersed within the continuous water phase without causing any separation.
- **Water-in-Oil (W/O) Emulsion:** If the emulsion breaks or separates upon the addition of water, it suggests that the continuous phase is oil. The added water does not mix with the continuous oil phase, leading to the disruption of the emulsion's stability. As a result, the emulsion may separate into distinct oil and water layers, with water droplets coalescing and separating from the oil phase.

Importance and Application: The dilution test is simple and effective for quickly identifying the type of emulsion, especially in settings where advanced equipment may not be available. It is widely used in pharmaceutical and cosmetic industries to ensure the correct formulation of products.

2. Dye Solubility Test:

Principle: The dye solubility test utilizes water-soluble and oil-soluble dyes to identify the continuous phase of an emulsion. This method is based on the differential solubility of dyes in the respective phases of the emulsion.

Procedure:

- **Step 1:** Select a water-soluble dye, such as methylene blue.
- **Step 2:** Add a small amount of this dye to a sample of the emulsion.
- **Step 3:** Stir gently and observe the mixture either visually or under a microscope.
- **Alternative:**

  - **Step 1:** Use an oil-soluble dye, such as Sudan III.
  - **Step 2:** Add the dye to a small amount of the emulsion.
  - **Step 3:** Observe the dispersion of the dye within the emulsion.

Interpretation:

- **Oil-in-Water (O/W) Emulsion:** If the water-soluble dye (e.g., methylene blue) disperses uniformly throughout the emulsion, it indicates that the continuous phase is water, meaning the emulsion is O/W. Conversely, if using an oil-soluble dye (e.g., Sudan III) and the dye does not disperse well or forms clumps, it confirms the O/W emulsion.
- **Water-in-Oil (W/O) Emulsion:** If the water-soluble dye forms clumps or does not disperse uniformly, it indicates that the continuous phase is oil, meaning the emulsion is W/O. Alternatively, if the oil-soluble dye disperses uniformly, it suggests a W/O emulsion.

Importance and Application: This test is particularly useful in the cosmetic and pharmaceutical industries, where understanding the continuous phase is crucial for predicting the behavior and stability of the emulsion. For instance, in the formulation of sunscreens, identifying the emulsion type helps in determining the spreadability and water resistance of the product.

3. Conductivity Test:

Principle: The conductivity test is based on the fact that water is a good conductor of electricity, while oil is not. Measuring the electrical conductivity of an emulsion can help determine the type of continuous phase.

Procedure:

- **Step 1:** Prepare the emulsion sample for testing.
- **Step 2:** Insert the probes of a conductivity meter into the emulsion.
- **Step 3:** Record the conductivity reading displayed by the meter.

Interpretation:

- **Oil-in-Water (O/W) Emulsion:** A high conductivity reading suggests that the continuous phase is water, which conducts electricity well. This indicates an O/W emulsion.
- **Water-in-Oil (W/O) Emulsion:** A low conductivity reading suggests that the continuous phase is oil, which does not conduct electricity well. This indicates a W/O emulsion.

Importance and Application: The conductivity test is a reliable and straightforward method for identifying emulsion types, especially useful in quality control settings. In the food industry, this test can help determine the type of emulsions used in products like salad dressings and sauces, ensuring consistency and quality.

4. Drop Test:

Principle: The drop test observes the behavior of a drop of emulsion when placed in water or oil. This simple test can indicate the type of emulsion based on whether the drop disperses or remains intact.

Procedure:

- **Step 1:** Take a small drop of the emulsion to be tested.
- **Step 2:** Place the drop into a container of water.
- **Step 3:** Observe the behavior of the drop.

Interpretation:

- **Oil-in-Water (O/W) Emulsion:** If the drop of emulsion disperses or spreads out in the water, it indicates an O/W emulsion, as the continuous water phase mixes readily with the surrounding water.

- **Water-in-Oil (W/O) Emulsion:** If the drop of emulsion remains intact or forms a distinct layer without dispersing, it indicates a W/O emulsion, as the continuous oil phase does not mix with the water.

Importance and Application: The drop test is a quick and easy method for identifying emulsion types, often used in preliminary formulation studies. It is particularly useful in the cosmetic industry, where understanding the emulsion type helps in developing products with desired textures and application properties.

5. Fluorescence Test:

Principle: Many oils exhibit fluorescence under ultraviolet light. This test utilizes this property to differentiate between O/W and W/O emulsions.

Procedure:

- **Step 1:** Place a sample of the emulsion under a UV light.
- **Step 2:** Observe the fluorescence pattern.

Interpretation:

- **Oil-in-Water (O/W) Emulsion:** If the dispersed phase fluoresces under UV light, it indicates that the oil droplets are dispersed in a continuous aqueous phase.
- **Water-in-Oil (W/O) Emulsion:** If the continuous phase fluoresces, it indicates that the oil phase is continuous with water droplets dispersed within it.

Importance and Application: The fluorescence test is highly useful in research and development settings where detailed analysis of emulsion characteristics is required. It is commonly used in pharmaceutical and cosmetic formulations to ensure proper phase distribution and stability.

6. Coagulation Test:

Principle: The addition of electrolytes can destabilize certain types of emulsions, causing them to coagulate or separate.

Procedure:

- **Step 1:** Add a small amount of an electrolyte (e.g., sodium chloride) to the emulsion.
- **Step 2:** Stir gently and observe for any signs of coagulation or phase separation.

Interpretation:

- **Oil-in-Water (O/W) Emulsions:** These emulsions are more likely to coagulate in the presence of electrolytes due to the increased ionic strength destabilizing the emulsion.
- **Water-in-Oil (W/O) Emulsions:** These emulsions are less likely to coagulate with the addition of electrolytes, as the continuous oil phase provides a barrier to ionic interactions.

Importance and Application: The coagulation test is particularly important in the formulation of emulsions where ionic interactions can affect stability, such as in pharmaceuticals and food products. Understanding how electrolytes impact emulsion stability can guide the selection of appropriate additives and preservatives.

7. Refractive Index Test:

Principle: The refractive index test measures the refractive index of the emulsion to identify the continuous phase based on the differences between oil and water.

Procedure:

- **Step 1:** Measure the refractive index of the emulsion using a refractometer.
- **Step 2:** Compare the refractive index to known values of oil and water.

Interpretation:

- **Oil-in-Water (O/W) Emulsion:** If the refractive index is closer to that of water, it indicates an O/W emulsion.
- **Water-in-Oil (W/O) Emulsion:** If the refractive index is closer to that of oil, it indicates a W/O emulsion.

Importance and Application: This test is valuable in quality control and formulation development, providing a quick and accurate method to determine the continuous phase of emulsions.

8. Creaming and Sedimentation Test:

Principle: Observes the separation behavior of the emulsion over time, indicating the stability and type of emulsion based on the movement of droplets.

Procedure:

- Step 1. Allow the emulsion to stand undisturbed for a specified period.
- **Step 2:** Observe for creaming (upward movement of droplets) or sedimentation (downward movement of droplets).

Interpretation:

- **Oil-in-Water (O/W) Emulsions:** Typically show creaming due to the lower density of oil droplets rising to the top.
- **Water-in-Oil (W/O) Emulsions:** May show sedimentation if the dispersed aqueous phase is denser than the continuous oil phase.

Importance and Application: This test is useful in determining the stability of emulsions over time, guiding formulation adjustments to enhance product shelf life and performance.

9. Microscopic Examination:

Principle: Direct visualization of the emulsion's microstructure helps identify the type of emulsion by observing the distribution of droplets.

Procedure:

- **Step 1:** Place a small sample of the emulsion on a microscope slide.
- **Step 2:** Examine under a microscope.

Interpretation:

- **Oil-in-Water (O/W) Emulsions:** Show oil droplets dispersed in a continuous aqueous phase.
- **Water-in-Oil (W/O) Emulsions:** Show water droplets dispersed in a continuous oil phase.

Importance and Application: Microscopic examination is a detailed and precise method for analyzing emulsion structure, widely used in research and development to optimize formulations.

10. Centrifugation Test:

Principle: Uses centrifugal force to accelerate the separation of emulsion phases, allowing for easy identification of the continuous and dispersed phases.

Procedure:

- **Step 1:** Centrifuge a sample of the emulsion at a specified speed and duration.
- **Step 2:** Observe the separation of phases.

Interpretation:

- The separated phases can be examined to identify the continuous and dispersed phases, indicating the type of emulsion.

Importance and Application: The centrifugation test is effective for quickly identifying emulsion types and assessing their stability, particularly useful in quality control and formulation development.

11. Inversion Test:

Principle: Involves changing the emulsion type by altering the phase volume ratio, providing insights into the emulsion's stability and phase behavior.

Procedure:

- **Step 1:** Gradually add the dispersed phase to the emulsion while stirring.
- **Step 2:** Observe for phase inversion.

Interpretation:

- **Oil-in-Water (O/W) Emulsions:** Can invert to water-in-oil (W/O) emulsions when the volume of the oil phase exceeds a critical point, and vice versa.

Importance and Application: The inversion test is crucial for understanding the limits of emulsion stability and for developing formulations that can withstand changes in phase volume ratios without compromising stability.

By using a combination of these tests, pharmacists and researchers can accurately identify the type of emulsion, ensuring proper formulation and application in pharmaceutical and cosmetic products. These tests provide valuable insights into the characteristics and stability of emulsions, guiding the development of effective and reliable products.

Methods of Preparation of Emulsions

The preparation of emulsions involves several techniques to ensure the proper mixing and stabilization of the immiscible phases (oil and water) to form a stable, homogeneous product. The choice of method depends on the type of emulsion, the scale of production, and the desired properties of the final product. Below are common methods for the preparation of emulsions:

1. Dry Gum Method

Principle: This method involves triturating the oil with an emulsifying agent before adding water.

Procedure:

1. Mix the oil with the emulsifying agent (e.g., acacia) in a mortar.
2. Add the required amount of water all at once while triturating vigorously.
3. Continue triturating until a thick, creamy primary emulsion is formed.
4. Dilute the primary emulsion with the remaining water to the desired volume, triturating after each addition.

Application: Suitable for preparing primary emulsions where a small volume of emulsion is needed.

2. Wet Gum Method

Principle: In this method, the emulsifying agent is first mixed with water to form a mucilage before the oil is added.

Procedure:

1. Mix the emulsifying agent (e.g., acacia) with water in a mortar to form a mucilage.
2. Gradually add the oil to the mucilage while triturating continuously.
3. Continue triturating until a uniform emulsion is formed.
4. Dilute with the remaining water to the desired volume, triturating after each addition.

Application: Commonly used for preparing emulsions that require a higher proportion of water.

3. Bottle Method

Principle: This method involves shaking the ingredients together in a bottle to form an emulsion.

Procedure:

1. Place the oil, water, and emulsifying agent (e.g., acacia) in a bottle.
2. Cap the bottle and shake vigorously until a stable emulsion forms.

Application: Suitable for extemporaneous compounding in pharmacies, especially for small volumes of emulsions.

4. Mechanical Method

Principle: This method uses mechanical devices to achieve the mixing and dispersion of phases.

Types:

- **Homogenization**:

  - **Procedure**: Pass the mixture of oil, water, and emulsifying agent through a high-pressure homogenizer, which breaks down the droplets to a fine size and ensures uniform distribution.
  - **Application**: Used in large-scale production of emulsions, such as pharmaceutical emulsions and cosmetic products.

- **Colloid Mills**:

  - **Procedure**: The mixture is passed through a colloid mill, where it is subjected to shear forces that break down the droplets.
  - **Application**: Suitable for both small and large-scale production, providing high shear and efficient mixing.

- **Ultrasonication**:

  - **Procedure**: The mixture is subjected to ultrasonic waves, which create cavitation and break down the droplets to a fine size.
  - **Application**: Effective for producing nanoemulsions and microemulsions with fine droplet sizes.

5. Phase Inversion Method

Principle: This method involves changing the relative volumes of the oil and water phases to induce phase inversion, leading to the formation of the desired emulsion type.

Procedure:

1. Start with a high concentration of the internal phase (e.g., water in oil).
2. Gradually add the external phase (e.g., oil) while stirring continuously.
3. Phase inversion occurs, forming the desired emulsion (e.g., O/W or W/O).

Application: Useful for producing emulsions with fine droplet sizes and high stability.

6. In Situ Soap Method

Principle: This method involves the formation of soap (emulsifying agent) in situ by a chemical reaction between the oil phase and an alkaline solution.

Procedure:

1. Add an oil (e.g., oleic acid) and an alkaline solution (e.g., sodium hydroxide) together.
2. The chemical reaction forms soap, which acts as an emulsifying agent.
3. The resulting mixture forms a stable emulsion.

Application: Used in the preparation of emulsions where the emulsifying agent is formed during the process.

Example Formulation for O/W Emulsion: Calamine Lotion

Active Ingredients: Calamine (8%), Zinc Oxide (8%)

Emulsifying Agent: Bentonite magma

Vehicle: Purified water and glycerin

Procedure

Preparation of Bentonite Magma

1. **Mixing**: Combine bentonite with water to form a magma. Ensure thorough mixing to achieve a uniform consistency.

Preparation of the Emulsion

1. **Adding Active Ingredients**: Add calamine and zinc oxide to the bentonite magma and mix thoroughly until the powders are evenly dispersed.
2. **Incorporating Water**: Gradually add purified water while continuously stirring the mixture to form a uniform emulsion.
3. **Adding Glycerin**: Add glycerin to the mixture and continue stirring until a homogeneous lotion is formed.

Packaging

1. **Transfer**: Pour the prepared lotion into appropriate containers.
2. **Label**: Label the containers with the necessary information, including the product name, ingredients, and usage instructions.

Stability Problems and Solutions in Emulsions

Emulsions, being biphasic liquid systems, face several stability challenges. Ensuring the stability of emulsions is crucial to maintain their effectiveness, shelf life, and safety. Below are common stability problems associated with emulsions and strategies to mitigate them:

1. Creaming

Definition: Creaming is the upward or downward movement of dispersed droplets within an emulsion, leading to the formation of a concentrated layer (cream) at the top or bottom.

Problem: Creaming indicates instability and can result in uneven distribution of the active ingredient, although it is usually reversible.

Solution:

- **Reduce Particle Size**: Smaller droplets reduce the rate of creaming.
- **Increase Viscosity**: Add viscosity enhancers like gums or polymers (e.g., xanthan gum, carbomers) to the continuous phase.
- **Density Matching**: Adjust the densities of the continuous and dispersed phases to be more similar, reducing the tendency to cream.

2. Coalescence

Definition: Coalescence is the merging of dispersed droplets to form larger droplets, eventually leading to phase separation.

Problem: Coalescence is irreversible and results in the breakdown of the emulsion.

Solution:

- **Use of Emulsifiers:** Effective emulsifiers stabilize the droplets by forming a protective layer around them (e.g., lecithin, Tween 80).
- **Increase Emulsifier Concentration:** Ensure an adequate amount of emulsifier to stabilize the droplet interface.
- **Add Stabilizers:** Incorporate stabilizers like polymers or surfactants that provide steric or electrostatic stabilization.

3. Phase Separation (Breaking or Cracking)

Definition: Phase separation occurs when the continuous and dispersed phases separate completely, leading to two distinct layers.

Problem: This indicates complete instability and renders the emulsion unusable.

Solution:

- **Optimize Emulsifier Selection:** Use a combination of emulsifiers to achieve better stability.
- **Control Environmental Conditions:** Store emulsions under optimal conditions (e.g., avoid temperature extremes).
- **Proper Formulation:** Ensure the correct ratio of oil to water phases and the appropriate type and concentration of emulsifiers.

4. Flocculation

Definition: Flocculation is the aggregation of droplets without coalescence, leading to the formation of flocs.

Problem: While flocculation is reversible, it can lead to uneven dosing and instability over time.

Solution:

- **Adjust pH and Electrolytes:** Optimize the pH and electrolyte concentration to minimize attractive forces between droplets.
- **Use Stabilizers:** Add stabilizers like polymers or surfactants to provide steric or electrostatic repulsion between droplets.

5. Ostwald Ripening

Definition: Ostwald ripening is the process where smaller droplets dissolve and redeposit onto larger droplets, leading to an increase in droplet size over time.

Problem: This results in instability and potential phase separation.
Solution:

- **Add Ripening Inhibitors**: Incorporate substances that inhibit the transfer of molecules between droplets (e.g., glycerol, propylene glycol).
- **Control Droplet Size Distribution**: Achieve a uniform droplet size distribution to minimize differences in solubility between droplets.

6. Microbial Contamination

Definition: Emulsions, particularly those with an aqueous phase, are susceptible to microbial growth.
Problem: Contamination can lead to spoilage and pose health risks.
Solution:

- **Use Preservatives**: Add suitable preservatives (e.g., parabens, benzyl alcohol) to prevent microbial growth.
- **Aseptic Processing**: Ensure aseptic conditions during manufacturing and packaging.
- **Proper Storage**: Store emulsions under conditions that minimize the risk of contamination (e.g., refrigeration if necessary).

7. Chemical Instability

Definition: Chemical instability involves the degradation of the active ingredient or emulsifiers over time.
Problem: This can reduce the efficacy and safety of the emulsion.
Solution:

- **Use Antioxidants**: Incorporate antioxidants (e.g., ascorbic acid, tocopherols) to prevent oxidation.
- **Optimize pH**: Adjust the pH to a range that maximizes the stability of the active ingredient and emulsifiers.
- **Protect from Light and Air**: Use opaque containers and airtight packaging to protect the emulsion from light and oxygen.

CHAPTER TEN

Suppositories

Definition and Types

Basic Definition
Suppositories:

- **Definition**: Suppositories are solid dosage forms intended for insertion into body orifices where they melt, soften, or dissolve to exert local or systemic effects. They are commonly used for rectal, vaginal, or urethral administration.
- **Composition**: Typically, suppositories are composed of an active pharmaceutical ingredient (API) embedded in a base that ensures the drug's release at body temperature. Common bases include cocoa butter (theobroma oil), polyethylene glycols (PEGs), glycerinated gelatin, and hydrogenated vegetable oils.

Explanation of Suppositories as a Dosage Form
Suppositories are designed to deliver medications directly to the site of action or for systemic absorption via mucous membranes. They offer an alternative route of administration when oral or parenteral delivery is impractical or unsuitable, such as in patients experiencing nausea, vomiting, or difficulties swallowing.

Advantages:

- **Local Treatment**: Direct delivery to the site of action, such as anti-inflammatory agents for rectal or vaginal inflammation.
- **Systemic Absorption**: Bypassing the gastrointestinal tract and avoiding first-pass metabolism, enhancing bioavailability of certain drugs.

- **Ease of Administration**: Suitable for patients unable to take oral medications.

Various Types of Suppositories

Rectal Suppositories
Therapeutic Uses and Benefits:

- **Therapeutic Uses**: Rectal suppositories are commonly used for local treatment of hemorrhoids, rectal inflammation, and as laxatives. They are also used for systemic effects, such as antipyretics (e.g., acetaminophen), antiemetics (e.g., promethazine), and analgesics (e.g., morphine).
- **Benefits**: Provide rapid relief for local conditions, bypass first-pass metabolism for systemic drugs, and can be administered to unconscious or vomiting patients.

Vaginal Suppositories
Applications and Advantages:

- **Applications**: Vaginal suppositories are used to treat local infections (e.g., antifungal agents for yeast infections), hormonal therapies (e.g., estrogen for menopause symptoms), and as contraceptives (e.g., spermicides).
- **Advantages**: Direct delivery to the site of infection or action, reduced systemic side effects, and improved patient compliance for chronic therapies.

Urethral Suppositories
Specific Uses and Administration:

- **Specific Uses**: Urethral suppositories, also known as bougies, are used primarily for local treatment of conditions like erectile dysfunction (e.g., alprostadil) and to deliver antibacterial agents for urinary tract infections.
- **Administration**: These are inserted into the urethra, where they dissolve and release the active ingredient directly to the target area, providing

effective local treatment.

Detailed Examples of Each Type
1. Rectal Suppositories
Example:

- **Active Ingredient**: Bisacodyl
- **Base**: Cocoa butter
- **Use**: As a stimulant laxative for relief of constipation.

Preparation:

1. **Weighing**: Accurately weigh the required amount of bisacodyl.
2. **Melting**: Melt the cocoa butter base using a water bath.
3. **Mixing**: Incorporate the bisacodyl into the molten base, ensuring uniform distribution.
4. **Molding**: Pour the mixture into suppository molds.
5. **Cooling**: Allow the suppositories to cool and solidify.
6. **Packaging**: Remove from molds and package in foil or plastic wrappers.

2. Vaginal Suppositories
Example:

- **Active Ingredient**: Clotrimazole
- **Base**: Polyethylene glycol (PEG)
- **Use**: For the treatment of vaginal yeast infections.

Preparation:

1. **Weighing**: Accurately weigh the required amount of clotrimazole.
2. **Melting**: Melt the PEG base at a controlled temperature.
3. **Mixing**: Homogeneously mix clotrimazole into the molten base.
4. **Molding**: Pour the mixture into vaginal suppository molds.
5. **Cooling**: Let the suppositories cool and solidify.
6. **Packaging**: Remove from molds and package appropriately.

3. Urethral Suppositories
Example:

- **Active Ingredient**: Alprostadil
- **Base**: Glycerinated gelatin
- **Use**: For the treatment of erectile dysfunction.

Preparation:

1. **Weighing**: Accurately weigh the required amount of alprostadil.
2. **Melting**: Prepare the glycerinated gelatin base by melting gelatin and glycerin in water.
3. **Mixing**: Dissolve alprostadil in the gelatin base while stirring.
4. **Molding**: Pour the mixture into urethral suppository molds.
5. **Cooling**: Allow the suppositories to cool and solidify.
6. **Packaging**: Carefully remove from molds and package in sterile containers.

Types of Bases

Oleaginous Bases
    Properties and Examples
    Properties:

- **Hydrophobic Nature**: Oleaginous bases are water-insoluble and do not mix with water.
- **Melting Point**: They have melting points close to body temperature, allowing the suppository to melt upon insertion.
- **Emollient Effect**: These bases provide a soothing effect and protect the mucous membranes.

Examples:

- **Cocoa Butter (Theobroma Oil)**: A natural fat that melts at body temperature and is commonly used for its smooth texture and ease of molding.
- **Hydrogenated Vegetable Oils**: Such as Witepsol and Suppocire, which are modified vegetable oils designed to have specific melting points and physical properties.

- **Fattibase**: A pre-blended suppository base that contains triglycerides and has consistent melting characteristics.

Water-Soluble and Water-Miscible Bases
Characteristics and Uses
Characteristics:

- **Hydrophilic Nature**: These bases are either soluble or dispersible in water, making them easy to clean and non-greasy.
- **Consistency**: They can be formulated to have various consistencies, from firm to soft, depending on the proportion of components used.
- **Compatibility**: Generally compatible with a wide range of drugs and less likely to cause sensitization or irritation.

Examples:

- **Polyethylene Glycols (PEGs)**: Available in various molecular weights, PEGs can be mixed to achieve the desired melting point and consistency. They are non-greasy and dissolve in body fluids.
- **Glycerinated Gelatin**: A mixture of gelatin, glycerin, and water used mainly for vaginal and urethral suppositories due to its soft consistency and good mucosal adhesion.

Uses:

- **Rectal Suppositories**: PEG bases are often used for rectal suppositories where a firm consistency and ease of administration are needed.
- **Vaginal Suppositories**: Glycerinated gelatin is preferred for its mucosal adhesion and soothing effect, making it suitable for vaginal use.
- **Urethral Suppositories**: The soft and dissolvable nature of glycerinated gelatin makes it ideal for urethral applications.

Selection Criteria and Properties
Factors Influencing Base Selection
1. Drug Compatibility:

- **Chemical Stability**: The base should not react with the active pharmaceutical ingredient (API) and should maintain the stability of the drug.

- **Solubility**: The solubility of the drug in the base affects its release profile. Hydrophilic drugs are better suited for oleaginous bases, while lipophilic drugs are better suited for water-soluble bases.

2. Desired Release Profile:

- **Immediate vs. Sustained Release**: Oleaginous bases tend to provide a slower, more sustained release, while water-soluble bases can provide a faster release of the drug.

3. Site of Administration:

- **Rectal**: Requires a base that melts at body temperature and provides a non-irritating, soothing effect.
- **Vaginal**: Prefers a base that adheres well to mucous membranes and provides comfort.
- **Urethral**: Needs a base that is soft, non-irritating, and dissolves completely.

4. Patient Comfort and Preference:

- **Ease of Insertion**: The base should allow for easy insertion without causing discomfort.
- **Residue**: Water-soluble bases tend to leave less residue and are easier to clean.

5. Manufacturing Considerations:

- **Molding and Solidification**: The base should be easy to mold and solidify into the desired shape and size.
- **Stability**: The base should maintain its physical and chemical stability during storage and use.

Practical Examples
Example 1: Oleaginous Base for Rectal Suppository Formulation:

- **Active Ingredient**: Acetaminophen
- **Base**: Cocoa butter

Preparation:

1. **Melting**: Melt the cocoa butter base using a water bath.
2. **Incorporation**: Incorporate the acetaminophen into the molten base, ensuring uniform distribution.
3. **Molding**: Pour the mixture into rectal suppository molds.
4. **Cooling**: Allow the suppositories to cool and solidify.
5. **Packaging**: Remove from molds and package in appropriate containers.

Example 2: Water-Soluble Base for Vaginal Suppository Formulation:

- **Active Ingredient**: Metronidazole
- **Base**: Glycerinated gelatin

Preparation:

1. **Melting**: Prepare the glycerinated gelatin base by melting gelatin and glycerin in water.
2. **Incorporation**: Dissolve metronidazole in the gelatin base while stirring.
3. **Molding**: Pour the mixture into vaginal suppository molds.
4. **Cooling**: Allow the suppositories to cool and solidify.
5. **Packaging**: Carefully remove from molds and package in sterile containers.

Conclusion

The selection of an appropriate suppository base is critical for the formulation's stability, efficacy, and patient comfort. Oleaginous bases like cocoa butter provide a soothing effect and are ideal for rectal use, while water-soluble bases like PEGs and glycerinated gelatin offer versatility and are suitable for various administration routes. Understanding the properties and selection criteria of different bases ensures the development of effective and patient-friendly suppository formulations tailored to specific therapeutic needs.

Methods of Preparation

Molding Method
Step-by-Step Process and Equipment
The molding method, also known as the fusion or pour-molding method, is a widely used technique for preparing suppositories. This method involves melting the base, incorporating the drug, and pouring the mixture into molds where it solidifies.
Step-by-Step Process:

1. **Weighing:**

   - Accurately weigh the required amounts of the active pharmaceutical ingredient (API) and the base.

2. **Melting the Base:**

   - **Equipment:** Water bath or melting apparatus.
   - **Process:** Place the base (e.g., cocoa butter, PEG) in a melting apparatus and heat it gently until it melts completely. Ensure the temperature is controlled to prevent degradation of heat-sensitive ingredients.

3. **Incorporation of API:**

   - **Equipment:** Stirring rod or mechanical stirrer.
   - **Process:** Gradually add the API to the molten base while stirring continuously to ensure uniform distribution. If the API is heat-sensitive, it should be dissolved or dispersed in a small amount of melted base or other suitable solvent before being added to the main batch.

4. **Pouring into Molds:**

   - **Equipment:** Suppository molds (metal, plastic, or silicone).
   - **Process:** Pour the homogeneous mixture into pre-lubricated or non-stick molds. Fill the molds slightly over the brim to allow for contraction during cooling.

5. **Cooling and Solidification:**

   - **Equipment**: Cooling chamber or refrigerator.
   - **Process**: Allow the filled molds to cool at room temperature or in a refrigerator until the suppositories solidify completely.

6. **Trimming and Packaging:**

   - **Equipment**: Trimming knife or spatula.
   - **Process**: Trim any excess base from the top of the molds to ensure uniform size and shape. Carefully remove the suppositories from the molds.
   - **Packaging**: Package the suppositories in appropriate containers, such as blister packs or foil wrappers, to protect them from moisture and contamination.

Advantages:

- Simple and straightforward process.
- Suitable for heat-stable APIs.
- Allows for precise dosing and uniform distribution of the API.

Disadvantages:

- Not suitable for heat-sensitive APIs.
- Requires careful temperature control to prevent degradation of the base and API.

Compression Method

The compression method is an alternative technique used for preparing suppositories, particularly when the API is sensitive to heat or when a high melting point base is used. This method involves compressing the base and API mixture into the desired shape.

Step-by-Step Process:

1. **Weighing:**

- Accurately weigh the required amounts of the API and the base.

2. **Powdering the Base:**

   - **Equipment**: Mill or grinder.
   - **Process**: Grind the base (e.g., hydrogenated vegetable oil, polyethylene glycol) into a fine powder to facilitate uniform mixing with the API.

3. **Mixing:**

   - **Equipment**: Mortar and pestle or mechanical mixer.
   - **Process**: Blend the powdered base with the API thoroughly to ensure a uniform mixture. This can be done manually using a mortar and pestle or mechanically using a mixer.

4. **Lubricating the Compression Mold:**

   - **Equipment**: Lubricant (e.g., vegetable oil, silicone spray).
   - **Process**: Apply a thin layer of lubricant to the compression mold to prevent sticking and facilitate easy removal of the suppositories.

5. **Filling the Compression Mold:**

   - **Equipment**: Suppository compression mold and machine.
   - **Process**: Fill the mold cavities with the powder mixture, ensuring they are evenly filled and packed.

6. **Compression:**

   - **Equipment**: Suppository compression machine.
   - **Process**: Compress the filled mold cavities using a suppository compression machine. This applies pressure to form the mixture into solid, uniformly shaped suppositories.

7. **Ejection and Packaging:**

   - **Equipment**: Ejection mechanism or manual removal tool.

- **Process**: Eject the compressed suppositories from the mold.
- **Packaging**: Package the suppositories in appropriate containers to protect them from moisture and contamination.

Advantages:

- Suitable for heat-sensitive APIs.
- Provides uniform suppository shapes and sizes.
- No need for melting, reducing the risk of API degradation.

Disadvantages:

- Requires specialized equipment for compression.
- May not be suitable for bases that do not compress well.

The molding and compression methods are both effective techniques for preparing suppositories, each with its own advantages and limitations. The molding method is simple and suitable for heat-stable APIs, while the compression method is ideal for heat-sensitive APIs and provides uniform suppository shapes without the need for melting. Understanding these methods allows pharmacists to select the appropriate technique based on the specific requirements of the formulation and the properties of the API. By following detailed preparation steps and using the correct equipment, high-quality suppositories can be produced to meet therapeutic needs.

Methods of Preparation

Molding Method

Step-by-Step Process and Equipment

The molding method involves melting the base, incorporating the active pharmaceutical ingredient (API), and pouring the mixture into molds where it solidifies.

Step-by-Step Process:

1. **Weighing**:

   - Accurately weigh the required amounts of the API and the base.

2. **Melting the Base**:

- **Equipment**: Water bath or melting apparatus.
- **Process**: Place the base (e.g., cocoa butter, polyethylene glycol) in a melting apparatus and heat gently until completely melted. Ensure the temperature is controlled to prevent degradation of the base and API.

3. **Incorporation of API**:

- **Equipment**: Stirring rod or mechanical stirrer.
- **Process**: Gradually add the API to the molten base while stirring continuously to ensure uniform distribution. If the API is heat-sensitive, it should be dissolved or dispersed in a small amount of melted base or another suitable solvent before being added to the main batch.

4. **Pouring into Molds**:

- **Equipment**: Suppository molds (metal, plastic, or silicone).
- **Process**: Pour the homogeneous mixture into pre-lubricated or non-stick molds. Fill the molds slightly over the brim to allow for contraction during cooling.

5. **Cooling and Solidification**:

- **Equipment**: Cooling chamber or refrigerator.
- **Process**: Allow the filled molds to cool at room temperature or in a refrigerator until the suppositories solidify completely.

6. **Trimming and Packaging**:

- **Equipment**: Trimming knife or spatula.
- **Process**: Trim any excess base from the top of the molds to ensure uniform size and shape. Carefully remove the suppositories from the molds.
- **Packaging**: Package the suppositories in appropriate containers, such as blister packs or foil wrappers, to protect them from moisture and contamination.

Practical Considerations:

- **Temperature Control**: Maintain appropriate temperatures to prevent degradation of the base and API.
- **Mixing**: Ensure thorough mixing to achieve a uniform distribution of the API.
- **Mold Preparation**: Pre-lubricate molds to facilitate easy removal of suppositories.

Compression Method

The compression method involves compressing a mixture of the base and API into the desired shape using specialized equipment.

Step-by-Step Process:

1. **Weighing:**

   - Accurately weigh the required amounts of the API and the base.

2. **Powdering the Base:**

   - **Equipment**: Mill or grinder.
   - **Process**: Grind the base (e.g., hydrogenated vegetable oil, polyethylene glycol) into a fine powder to facilitate uniform mixing with the API.

3. **Mixing:**

   - **Equipment**: Mortar and pestle or mechanical mixer.
   - **Process**: Blend the powdered base with the API thoroughly to ensure a uniform mixture.

4. **Lubricating the Compression Mold:**

   - **Equipment**: Lubricant (e.g., vegetable oil, silicone spray).
   - **Process**: Apply a thin layer of lubricant to the compression mold to prevent sticking and facilitate easy removal of the suppositories.

5. **Filling the Compression Mold:**

- **Equipment**: Suppository compression mold and machine.
- **Process**: Fill the mold cavities with the powder mixture, ensuring they are evenly filled and packed.

6. **Compression**:

  - **Equipment**: Suppository compression machine.
  - **Process**: Compress the filled mold cavities using a suppository compression machine. This applies pressure to form the mixture into solid, uniformly shaped suppositories.

7. **Ejection and Packaging**:

  - **Equipment**: Ejection mechanism or manual removal tool.
  - **Process**: Eject the compressed suppositories from the mold.
  - **Packaging**: Package the suppositories in appropriate containers to protect them from moisture and contamination.

Practical Considerations:

- **Uniform Mixing**: Ensure the base and API are thoroughly mixed to achieve consistent dosing.
- **Compression Pressure**: Adjust the pressure to achieve the desired suppository hardness and shape.
- **Mold Lubrication**: Proper lubrication is essential to prevent sticking and ensure easy removal.

Hand Rolling Method

The hand rolling method is a traditional and manual technique used to prepare suppositories, particularly when only a small quantity is required or when specialized equipment is not available.

Manual Preparation Techniques:

Step-by-Step Process:

1. **Weighing**:

  - Accurately weigh the required amounts of the API and the base.

2. **Preparation of the Base:**

- **Equipment**: Mortar and pestle or mixing bowl.
- **Process**: Use a suitable base such as cocoa butter or a mixture of wax and oil. If the base is solid, soften it by gentle heating or kneading.

3. **Incorporation of API:**

- **Equipment**: Mortar and pestle or mixing spatula.
- **Process**: Thoroughly mix the API with the softened base to achieve a uniform mixture. This can be done manually using a mortar and pestle or a mixing spatula.

4. **Shaping the Suppositories:**

- **Equipment**: Hands, spatula, or rolling board.
- **Process**: Roll the mixture into a cylindrical shape with a diameter slightly larger than the final suppository. Cut the cylinder into equal-sized pieces, each representing one dose. Shape each piece into a conical or torpedo shape by hand.

5. **Cooling and Solidification:**

- **Equipment**: Cooling surface or refrigerator.
- **Process**: Place the shaped suppositories on a clean, cool surface or refrigerate them to allow them to harden.

6. **Packaging:**

- **Equipment**: Foil wrappers or plastic containers.
- **Process**: Once solidified, wrap each suppository in foil or place them in plastic containers to protect them from contamination and environmental factors.

Practical Considerations:

- **Uniform Mixing**: Ensure thorough mixing of the API with the base to achieve consistent dosing.

- **Shaping**: Aim for uniform size and shape to ensure accurate dosing and ease of administration.
- **Hygiene**: Maintain a clean work environment to prevent contamination.

Methods of Preparation

Practical Examples and Techniques
  1. Molding Method
  Case Study: Preparation of Rectal Suppositories for Pain Relief
  Objective: To prepare rectal suppositories containing acetaminophen for pain relief using the molding method.
  Ingredients:

- Active Ingredient: Acetaminophen (500 mg per suppository)
- Base: Cocoa butter (Theobroma oil)

  Step-by-Step Process:

1. **Weighing**:

   - Weigh 500 mg of acetaminophen per suppository.
   - Weigh the appropriate amount of cocoa butter (typically around 2 g per suppository, depending on the mold size).

2. **Melting the Base**:

   - Melt the cocoa butter in a water bath at a temperature just above its melting point (around 35°C).

3. **Incorporation of API**:

   - Gradually add the acetaminophen to the molten cocoa butter while stirring continuously to ensure uniform distribution.

4. **Pouring into Molds**:

   - Pour the mixture into pre-lubricated or non-stick suppository molds.

5. **Cooling and Solidification:**

- Allow the filled molds to cool at room temperature or refrigerate until the suppositories solidify.

6. **Trimming and Packaging:**

- Trim any excess base from the molds to ensure uniform size and shape.
- Carefully remove the suppositories from the molds and package them in foil wrappers.

Outcome:

- The prepared suppositories are uniform in size and contain the correct dose of acetaminophen. They provide effective pain relief when administered rectally.

2. Compression Method

Case Study: Preparation of Vaginal Suppositories for Antifungal Treatment

Objective: To prepare vaginal suppositories containing clotrimazole for the treatment of yeast infections using the compression method.

Ingredients:

- Active Ingredient: Clotrimazole (100 mg per suppository)
- Base: Polyethylene glycol (PEG) 1000 and PEG 4000 (60:40 ratio)

Step-by-Step Process:

1. **Weighing:**

- Weigh 100 mg of clotrimazole per suppository.
- Weigh the appropriate amounts of PEG 1000 and PEG 4000.

2. **Powdering the Base:**

- Grind the PEG 1000 and PEG 4000 into a fine powder.

3. **Mixing**:

- Blend the powdered base with the clotrimazole thoroughly using a mortar and pestle.

4. **Lubricating the Compression Mold**:

- Apply a thin layer of lubricant to the compression mold.

5. **Filling the Compression Mold**:

- Fill the mold cavities with the powder mixture.

6. **Compression**:

- Compress the filled mold cavities using a suppository compression machine.

7. **Ejection and Packaging**:

- Eject the compressed suppositories from the mold.
- Package the suppositories in sterile containers.

Outcome:

- The compressed suppositories are uniform and effective for treating vaginal yeast infections, providing relief from symptoms.

Hand Rolling Method
Case Study: Preparation of Urethral Suppositories for Erectile Dysfunction
Objective: To prepare urethral suppositories containing alprostadil using the hand rolling method.
Ingredients:

- Active Ingredient: Alprostadil (500 mcg per suppository)
- Base: Glycerinated gelatin

Step-by-Step Process:

1. **Weighing:**

   - Weigh 500 mcg of alprostadil per suppository.
   - Weigh the appropriate amount of glycerinated gelatin.

2. **Preparation of the Base:**

   - Soften the glycerinated gelatin base by gentle heating.

3. **Incorporation of API:**

   - Thoroughly mix the alprostadil with the softened base to achieve a uniform mixture.

4. **Shaping the Suppositories:**

   - Roll the mixture into a cylindrical shape with a diameter slightly larger than the final suppository.
   - Cut the cylinder into equal-sized pieces, each representing one dose.
   - Shape each piece into a conical or torpedo shape by hand.

5. **Cooling and Solidification:**

   - Place the shaped suppositories on a clean, cool surface or refrigerate them to allow them to harden.

6. **Packaging:**

   - Wrap each suppository in foil or place them in plastic containers to protect them from contamination and environmental factors.

   Outcome:

- The hand-rolled suppositories are effective for treating erectile dysfunction and are easy to administer.

These practical examples and case studies illustrate the application of different preparation methods for suppositories. Each method—molding, compression, and hand rolling—has specific steps and equipment requirements that ensure the production of high-quality suppositories tailored to the therapeutic needs of patients. By understanding and applying these techniques, pharmacists can create effective and safe suppository formulations for various medical conditions.

Displacement Value Calculations

Concept of Displacement Value
    Definition and Significance
    Displacement Value:

- **Definition**: The displacement value (DV) is a measure of the volume of suppository base displaced by a unit weight of the active pharmaceutical ingredient (API). It represents the ratio of the weight of the API to the volume it displaces in the suppository base.
- **Significance**: Understanding the displacement value is crucial in suppository formulation to ensure accurate dosing and uniformity. It allows for the correct adjustment of the base quantity when incorporating the API, ensuring each suppository contains the precise amount of active ingredient.

Importance:

- **Dosing Accuracy**: Accurate displacement values ensure that each suppository contains the intended dose of the API.
- **Uniformity**: Ensures consistent size and weight of suppositories, which is important for patient compliance and therapeutic efficacy.
- **Formulation Efficiency**: Helps in calculating the exact amount of base required, reducing wastage and optimizing the production process.

Calculation Methods
Step-by-Step Calculation Techniques
To calculate the displacement value, the following steps are typically involved:

1. **Determine the Weight of the Base:**

   - Prepare a batch of suppositories using only the base (without API) and determine the average weight of the base required to fill the mold.

2. **Incorporate the API:**

   - Prepare another batch of suppositories by incorporating a known weight of the API into the base. Ensure uniform mixing.

3. **Determine the Weight of the API:**

   - Measure the weight of the API added to the suppository formulation.

4. **Calculate the Weight of the Suppository with API:**

   - Measure the average weight of the suppositories containing the API.

5. **Calculate the Displacement Value:**

   - Use the formula to calculate the displacement value:

   ??=Weight of API addedWeight of base displacedDV=Weight of base displacedWeight of API added

   - The weight of the base displaced can be calculated as the difference between the weight of the suppository with API and the weight of the suppository with only the base.

Practical Examples and Problem-Solving

Sample Problem 1: Calculating the Displacement Value
   Problem:

- You are formulating a batch of rectal suppositories containing 300 mg of paracetamol (API) per suppository. The average weight of a suppository made with only the base (cocoa butter) is 2 g. After incorporating the API, the average weight of the suppositories is 2.1 g. Calculate the displacement value of paracetamol in cocoa butter.

Solution:

1. **Determine the Weight of the Base:**

   - Weight of base-only suppository = 2 g

2. **Incorporate the API:**

   - API weight per suppository = 300 mg = 0.3 g

3. **Calculate the Weight of the Suppository with API:**

   - Weight of suppository with API = 2.1 g

4. **Calculate the Weight of Base Displaced:**

   - Weight of base displaced = Weight of suppository with API - Weight of base-only suppository
   - Weight of base displaced = 2.1 g - 2 g = 0.1 g

5. **Calculate the Displacement Value:**

   - $DV = \dfrac{0.3\,g}{0.1\,g} = 3$

Interpretation:

- The displacement value of paracetamol in cocoa butter is 3, meaning 1 g of paracetamol displaces 3 g of the base.

Sample Problem 2: Adjusting the Base Quantity
Problem:

- You need to prepare 20 rectal suppositories containing 200 mg of ibuprofen per suppository. The displacement value of ibuprofen in the chosen base (Witepsol) is 1.5. Calculate the total amount of base required.

Solution:

1. **Calculate the Total Weight of API:**

   - Total weight of API = 200 mg/suppository × 20 suppositories
   - Total weight of API = 4000 mg = 4 g

2. **Calculate the Volume of Base Displaced by API:**

   - Volume of base displaced = Weight of API / DV
   - Volume of base displaced = 4 g / 1.5
   - Volume of base displaced = 2.67 g

3. **Determine the Total Weight of Suppositories without API:**

   - Assume the average weight of a suppository without API is 2 g.
   - Total weight of base-only suppositories = 2 g/suppository × 20 suppositories
   - Total weight of base-only suppositories = 40 g

4. **Calculate the Total Amount of Base Required:**

   - Total base required = Total weight of base-only suppositories - Volume of base displaced
   - Total base required = 40 g - 2.67 g
   - Total base required = 37.33 g

Interpretation:

- To prepare 20 suppositories containing 200 mg of ibuprofen each, you need 37.33 g of Witepsol base.

Evaluation of Suppositories

Quality Control Tests

Standards and Protocols

Evaluating the quality of suppositories is crucial to ensure their safety, efficacy, and patient acceptability. Quality control tests are conducted according to established standards and protocols set by pharmacopeias (e.g., USP, BP, IP).

1. Uniformity of Weight:

- **Protocol:** Weigh 20 individual suppositories and calculate the average weight. The individual weights should not deviate significantly from the average weight.
- **Standards:** According to pharmacopeial standards, no more than two suppositories should deviate from the average weight by more than 5%, and none should deviate by more than 10%.

2. Content Uniformity:

- **Protocol:** Determine the active ingredient content in 10 individual suppositories. Each suppository should contain the labeled amount of the active ingredient within a specified range.
- **Standards:** The content of the active ingredient should not deviate by more than 15% from the labeled amount in any individual suppository.

3. Melting Point:

- **Protocol:** Determine the melting point of the base or the suppository using a melting point apparatus. This ensures that the suppository melts at body temperature.
- **Standards:** The melting point should be close to body temperature ($37°C$) for rectal and vaginal suppositories.

4. Disintegration Test:

- **Protocol:** Place the suppository in a disintegration test apparatus with water or simulated body fluid at $37°C$ and observe the time taken for complete disintegration.
- **Standards:** Suppositories should disintegrate within a specified time, usually 30 minutes for rectal and vaginal suppositories.

5. Dissolution Test:

- **Protocol**: Use a dissolution apparatus to measure the rate and extent of drug release from the suppository in a specified medium at 37°C.
- **Standards**: The dissolution profile should meet the pharmacopeial specifications for the active ingredient.

Physical and Chemical Evaluation
Methods and Criteria
1. Appearance:

- **Method**: Visually inspect the suppositories for uniformity in shape, color, and the absence of cracks, fissures, or discoloration.
- **Criteria**: Suppositories should be smooth, uniform, and free from physical defects.

2. Hardness:

- **Method**: Measure the force required to break or deform the suppository using a hardness tester.
- **Criteria**: Suppositories should have sufficient hardness to withstand handling but should not be too hard to cause discomfort during administration.

3. Brittleness:

- **Method**: Test the suppositories for brittleness by subjecting them to a specific force or dropping them from a certain height.
- **Criteria**: Suppositories should not be brittle and should withstand handling without breaking.

4. pH Measurement:

- **Method**: Dissolve the suppository in water and measure the pH of the solution.
- **Criteria**: The pH should be within an acceptable range to avoid irritation of the mucosal membranes.

5. Chemical Assay:

- **Method**: Use appropriate analytical techniques (e.g., HPLC, UV spectroscopy) to quantify the active ingredient in the suppository.
- **Criteria**: The active ingredient content should be within the specified range, typically 90-110% of the labeled amount.

Clinical Efficacy and Patient Acceptability
Factors Influencing Efficacy and Acceptance
1. Drug Release and Bioavailability:

- **Factor**: The rate and extent of drug release from the suppository base can affect bioavailability.
- **Influence**: Formulations should ensure optimal drug release for effective therapy. Techniques like using appropriate bases, surfactants, and optimizing melting points can enhance drug release.

2. Comfort and Convenience:

- **Factor**: The ease of insertion, absence of irritation, and patient comfort are critical for acceptance.
- **Influence**: Suppositories should be smooth, non-irritating, and appropriately sized to ensure patient comfort and compliance. Glycerinated gelatin or PEG bases are often used to enhance comfort.

3. Stability and Storage:

- **Factor**: Stability of the suppositories during storage can impact efficacy and safety.
- **Influence**: Suppositories should maintain their physical and chemical integrity during storage. Proper packaging and storage conditions (e.g., refrigeration for heat-sensitive formulations) are essential.

4. Onset and Duration of Action:

- **Factor**: The time it takes for the drug to take effect and the duration of its action.

- **Influence**: Formulations should be designed to provide a rapid onset of action if required, or sustained release for prolonged effect. The choice of base and excipients can modulate the release profile.

5. Patient Education:

- **Factor**: Proper patient education on the use and administration of suppositories.
- **Influence**: Providing clear instructions on how to store, handle, and administer suppositories can improve compliance and therapeutic outcomes.

Practical Examples and Problem-Solving
Example 1: Evaluating a Rectal Suppository for Pain Relief
Quality Control Tests:

1. **Uniformity of Weight**: Weigh 20 suppositories containing 300 mg acetaminophen each. Ensure no more than two suppositories deviate by more than 5%, and none by more than 10%.
2. **Content Uniformity**: Analyze the active ingredient content in 10 suppositories to ensure each contains 300 mg ± 15%.
3. **Melting Point**: Determine the melting point of the base (cocoa butter) to ensure it melts at body temperature.
4. **Disintegration Test**: Verify the suppositories disintegrate within 30 minutes in simulated rectal fluid.
5. **Dissolution Test**: Measure the rate of acetaminophen release to ensure it meets the specified dissolution profile.

Example 2: Ensuring Patient Acceptability of Vaginal Suppositories for Antifungal Treatment
Patient Acceptability Factors:

1. **Comfort**: Ensure the suppositories are smooth and appropriately sized for easy insertion.
2. **Non-Irritating**: Use a pH-balanced base (glycerinated gelatin) to avoid mucosal irritation.
3. **Storage Stability**: Package the suppositories in moisture-proof containers and store them in a cool place to maintain stability.

CHAPTER ELEVEN

Pharmaceutical Incompatibilities

Definition and Classification

Basic Definition

Pharmaceutical Incompatibilities:

- **Definition**: Pharmaceutical incompatibilities refer to the undesirable reactions that occur between two or more components within a pharmaceutical preparation, leading to reduced efficacy, altered therapeutic effects, or potential harm to the patient. These reactions can occur during the formulation, compounding, storage, or administration of pharmaceutical products.

Explanation of Pharmaceutical Incompatibilities

Incompatibilities can manifest as physical changes (e.g., precipitation, color change), chemical reactions (e.g., hydrolysis, oxidation), or therapeutic issues (e.g., antagonistic drug interactions). Understanding and identifying incompatibilities is crucial for ensuring the stability, safety, and efficacy of pharmaceutical products.

Types of Incompatibilities

1. Physical Incompatibilities

Overview: Physical incompatibilities arise from physical interactions between components, leading to visible changes without altering the chemical nature of the substances involved.

Examples:

- **Precipitation**: Formation of solid particles in a solution, often seen when two solutions are mixed and the resultant product is insoluble.
- **Liquefaction**: Transformation of a solid to a liquid state, usually due to the interaction of two solids that form a eutectic mixture.
- **Color Change**: Visible alteration in color, indicating possible physical interaction between components.

Case Example:

- **Precipitation**: Mixing calcium chloride and sodium bicarbonate solutions results in the formation of insoluble calcium carbonate, precipitating out of the solution.

2. Chemical Incompatibilities

Overview: Chemical incompatibilities occur due to chemical reactions between components, resulting in the formation of new compounds that may be inactive, toxic, or otherwise undesirable.

Examples:

- **Hydrolysis**: Breakdown of a compound due to reaction with water.
- **Oxidation**: Loss of electrons from a substance, often leading to degradation.
- **Reduction**: Gain of electrons, potentially altering the chemical structure.
- **Complexation**: Formation of a complex between two or more substances, potentially altering their efficacy.

Case Example:

- **Hydrolysis**: Aspirin (acetylsalicylic acid) undergoes hydrolysis in the presence of moisture, producing salicylic acid and acetic acid, reducing its therapeutic efficacy.

3. Therapeutic Incompatibilities

Overview: Therapeutic incompatibilities arise when the combined effect of two or more drugs leads to reduced therapeutic efficacy or increased toxicity.

Examples:

- **Synergism**: Two drugs produce a combined effect greater than the sum of their individual effects, potentially leading to toxicity.
- **Antagonism**: One drug reduces or inhibits the effect of another, reducing therapeutic efficacy.
- **Altered Pharmacokinetics**: One drug affects the absorption, distribution, metabolism, or excretion of another, leading to suboptimal therapeutic outcomes.

Case Example:

- **Antagonism**: The combination of antacids (e.g., aluminum hydroxide) with tetracycline antibiotics reduces the absorption of tetracycline, decreasing its effectiveness.

Physical Incompatibilities

Causes and Examples

Physical incompatibilities occur when physical interactions between pharmaceutical components lead to undesirable changes in the formulation. These changes can affect the appearance, texture, and overall stability of the product without altering the chemical nature of the ingredients. Common causes of physical incompatibilities include differences in solubility, pH, and physical state of the components.

Common Physical Incompatibilities

1. Precipitation:

- **Cause**: When two solutions are mixed and an insoluble product forms, leading to precipitation.
- **Example**: Mixing calcium chloride and sodium bicarbonate solutions results in the formation of calcium carbonate, which precipitates out.

2. Liquefaction (Eutectic Mixtures):

- **Cause**: When two solid substances are mixed and form a liquid at room temperature due to the formation of a eutectic mixture.
- **Example**: Mixing camphor and menthol results in a eutectic mixture that liquefies at room temperature.

3. Color Change:

- **Cause**: Physical interaction between components leading to a visible change in color, indicating a potential incompatibility.
- **Example**: Mixing ferric chloride with tannic acid results in a deep blue-black color due to the formation of iron-tannate complex.

4. Gel Formation:

- **Cause**: Interaction between components that leads to the formation of a gel, altering the consistency and usability of the formulation.
- **Example**: Mixing sodium alginate with calcium chloride results in the formation of a gel-like substance due to cross-linking of alginate chains.

Prevention and Management Strategies

Techniques to Avoid Physical Incompatibilities
1. Understanding Solubility:

- **Strategy**: Ensure that all components are compatible in terms of solubility. Use solvents that can dissolve all active and inactive ingredients adequately.
- **Example**: When preparing an injectable solution, ensure that all salts used are soluble in the chosen solvent to avoid precipitation.

2. Adjusting pH:

- **Strategy**: Adjust the pH of the solution to maintain the solubility and stability of the components. Use buffers if necessary.
- **Example**: Adjusting the pH of an ampicillin solution to enhance its stability and prevent precipitation.

3. Avoiding Eutectic Mixtures:

- **Strategy**: Use excipients that prevent liquefaction or mix eutectic-forming substances with inert carriers to absorb the liquid formed.

- **Example**: Mixing eutectic substances like camphor and menthol with lactose to absorb the liquid and maintain a dry powder.

4. Proper Order of Mixing:

- **Strategy**: Add components in a specific order to prevent incompatibilities. For example, add the more soluble component first.
- **Example**: When preparing a suspension, add the suspending agent to the vehicle before incorporating the active ingredient to ensure proper dispersion.

5. Using Compatible Excipients:

- **Strategy**: Choose excipients that do not interact adversely with the active ingredients or other excipients.
- **Example**: Using non-ionic surfactants in emulsions to prevent precipitation and phase separation.

Case Studies
Case Study 1: Precipitation in Parenteral Nutrition Solution
Problem:

- A parenteral nutrition solution containing calcium gluconate and potassium phosphate showed precipitation after mixing.

Cause:

- The precipitation was due to the formation of insoluble calcium phosphate.

Management Strategy:

- **Solution**: Add calcium gluconate and potassium phosphate to the solution in a specific order and at the right concentrations to maintain solubility. Also, consider adjusting the pH to enhance solubility.

Outcome:

- The adjusted preparation protocol prevented precipitation, ensuring a stable and safe parenteral nutrition solution.

Case Study 2: Liquefaction in Powdered Formulation
Problem:

- A powdered formulation containing camphor and menthol liquefied upon mixing, forming a sticky mass.

Cause:

- Formation of a eutectic mixture due to the low melting point of the combined substances.

Management Strategy:

- **Solution**: Mix camphor and menthol with an inert carrier like lactose to absorb the liquid formed by the eutectic mixture.

Outcome:

- The modified formulation remained dry and free-flowing, avoiding the issue of liquefaction.

Case Study 3: Color Change in Topical Preparation
Problem:

- A topical preparation containing ferric chloride and tannic acid turned deep blue-black, indicating a potential incompatibility.

Cause:

- The color change was due to the formation of an iron-tannate complex.

Management Strategy:

- **Solution**: Formulate the components separately or use alternative ingredients that do not interact to form a colored complex.

Outcome:

- The reformulated preparation maintained its intended color and stability, avoiding the undesirable color change.

Chemical Incompatibilities

Mechanisms and Examples

Chemical reactions causing incompatibilities

Chemical incompatibilities occur when reactions between pharmaceutical components lead to changes in the chemical structure, resulting in reduced efficacy, altered therapeutic effects, or potential toxicity. Common mechanisms include hydrolysis, oxidation, reduction, and complexation.

1. Hydrolysis:

- **Mechanism**: Hydrolysis involves the reaction of a compound with water, leading to the breakdown of the molecule.
- **Example**: Aspirin (acetylsalicylic acid) hydrolyzes in the presence of moisture, forming salicylic acid and acetic acid, which reduces its efficacy and can cause irritation.

2. Oxidation:

- **Mechanism**: Oxidation involves the loss of electrons from a molecule, often leading to degradation.
- **Example**: Epinephrine is prone to oxidation, turning brown due to the formation of adrenochrome, which reduces its potency.

3. Reduction:

- **Mechanism**: Reduction involves the gain of electrons by a molecule, potentially altering its chemical structure.
- **Example**: Hydrogen peroxide, when exposed to reducing agents, decomposes into water and oxygen, losing its effectiveness as an antiseptic.

4. Complexation:

- **Mechanism**: Complexation involves the formation of a complex between two or more compounds, potentially inactivating the drug.
- **Example**: Tetracycline forms an insoluble complex with calcium ions, reducing its absorption and therapeutic efficacy.

Identification and Mitigation
Methods to detect and prevent chemical incompatibilities
1. Identifying Chemical Incompatibilities:

- **pH Measurement**: Monitor the pH of the formulation, as certain reactions are pH-dependent. For example, the stability of penicillin is pH-sensitive, and it degrades rapidly in acidic or basic conditions.
- **Color Change Observation**: Some chemical reactions cause a visible color change. For example, oxidation of ferrous sulfate results in a color change to ferric sulfate.
- **Precipitation Testing**: Look for precipitation or turbidity in solutions, which can indicate complexation or degradation. For example, the formation of a precipitate when calcium and phosphate salts are mixed in parenteral nutrition solutions.
- **Analytical Techniques**: Use techniques such as High-Performance Liquid Chromatography (HPLC), Gas Chromatography (GC), and Mass Spectrometry (MS) to detect degradation products and confirm chemical compatibility.

2. Mitigating Chemical Incompatibilities:

- **Buffering Agents**: Use buffering agents to maintain a stable pH. For instance, adding a phosphate buffer to maintain the stability of penicillin.
- **Antioxidants**: Incorporate antioxidants like ascorbic acid or sodium metabisulfite to prevent oxidation. For example, adding ascorbic acid to formulations containing epinephrine.
- **Chelating Agents**: Use chelating agents like EDTA to bind metal ions that can catalyze degradation reactions. For example, adding EDTA to tetracycline formulations to prevent complexation with calcium.
- **Protective Packaging**: Use packaging that protects from light, moisture, and air, such as amber glass bottles for light-sensitive drugs like

riboflavin.

- **Inert Atmosphere**: Store and package products in an inert atmosphere (e.g., nitrogen) to prevent oxidative degradation. For example, using nitrogen flushing for injectable solutions prone to oxidation.

Case Studies
Practical examples and solutions
Case Study 1: Hydrolysis of Aspirin
Problem:

- Aspirin tablets stored in humid conditions exhibited a vinegar-like smell, indicating hydrolysis.

Cause:

- Exposure to moisture led to the hydrolysis of aspirin into salicylic acid and acetic acid.

Mitigation:

- **Solution**: Store aspirin tablets in airtight, moisture-proof containers with desiccants to absorb moisture.

Outcome:

- The use of moisture-proof packaging prevented hydrolysis, maintaining the efficacy of the aspirin tablets.

Case Study 2: Oxidation of Epinephrine
Problem:

- Epinephrine injections turned brown, indicating oxidation and reduced potency.

Cause:

- Exposure to air and light caused the oxidation of epinephrine.

Mitigation:

- **Solution:** Add an antioxidant (e.g., ascorbic acid) and store the injections in amber glass ampoules to protect from light and air.

Outcome:

- The addition of an antioxidant and protective packaging prevented oxidation, preserving the potency of the epinephrine injections.

Case Study 3: Complexation of Tetracycline
Problem:

- Tetracycline capsules taken with milk resulted in reduced therapeutic effectiveness.

Cause:

- Tetracycline formed an insoluble complex with calcium in the milk, reducing its absorption.

Mitigation:

- **Solution:** Advise patients to avoid taking tetracycline with dairy products and to take it with water instead.

Outcome:

- Patient education on proper administration improved the absorption and efficacy of tetracycline.

Case Study 4: Precipitation in Parenteral Nutrition
Problem:

- Precipitation observed in parenteral nutrition solutions containing calcium and phosphate.

Cause:

- Incompatibility between calcium and phosphate leading to the formation of insoluble calcium phosphate.

Mitigation:

- **Solution**: Adjust the concentrations and order of mixing of calcium and phosphate, and use a buffer to maintain solubility.

Outcome:

- Careful formulation adjustments prevented precipitation, ensuring the stability and safety of the parenteral nutrition solution.

Therapeutic Incompatibilities

Definitions and Examples
   Therapeutic Incompatibilities:

- **Definition**: Therapeutic incompatibilities occur when the combined effect of two or more drugs leads to reduced therapeutic efficacy, enhanced toxicity, or altered pharmacokinetic profiles. These interactions can impact the overall therapeutic outcome and patient safety.

Examples:

1. **Synergism:**

   - **Example**: Combining two central nervous system (CNS) depressants like benzodiazepines (e.g., diazepam) and alcohol can lead to excessive sedation, respiratory depression, and even death due to the additive depressant effects.

2. **Antagonism:**

   - **Example**: The concurrent use of beta-blockers (e.g., propranolol) and beta-agonists (e.g., albuterol) can result in reduced effectiveness of the beta-agonist in treating asthma, as the beta-blocker inhibits the action of the beta-agonist.

3. **Altered Pharmacokinetics:**

- **Example:** The use of antacids containing aluminum hydroxide or magnesium hydroxide can decrease the absorption of tetracycline antibiotics, leading to subtherapeutic levels and reduced efficacy.

Clinical Significance
Impact on Patient Care
Therapeutic incompatibilities can have significant clinical implications, affecting patient safety and treatment outcomes. Some key impacts include:

1. **Reduced Efficacy:**

- Incompatibilities can lead to subtherapeutic drug levels, rendering treatments less effective. For example, the interaction between antacids and tetracyclines can lead to inadequate antibiotic coverage and persistent infections.

2. **Enhanced Toxicity:**

- Drug interactions can increase the risk of adverse effects. For instance, combining two hepatotoxic drugs (e.g., acetaminophen and isoniazid) can elevate the risk of liver damage.

3. **Increased Adverse Effects:**

- Therapeutic incompatibilities can exacerbate side effects, leading to increased discomfort and risk for the patient. An example is the combined use of anticoagulants (e.g., warfarin) with nonsteroidal anti-inflammatory drugs (NSAIDs), which can increase the risk of gastrointestinal bleeding.

4. **Altered Drug Action:**

- Interactions can alter the intended pharmacological action, making management of the patient's condition more challenging. For example, using a diuretic (e.g., furosemide) with a non-steroidal anti-inflammatory drug (NSAID) can reduce the diuretic effect, complicating the management of conditions like hypertension and heart failure.

Management Approaches
Strategies to Manage Therapeutic Incompatibilities

1. **Medication Review and Reconciliation**:

   - **Approach**: Conduct a thorough review of all medications the patient is taking, including prescription, over-the-counter, and herbal supplements, to identify potential incompatibilities.
   - **Example**: Regularly updating the patient's medication list and cross-checking for interactions using drug interaction databases or tools.

2. **Patient Education**:

   - **Approach**: Educate patients about the potential interactions between their medications and the importance of following dosing instructions.
   - **Example**: Advising patients to avoid alcohol while taking CNS depressants to prevent excessive sedation and respiratory depression.

3. **Therapeutic Drug Monitoring**:

   - **Approach**: Monitor drug levels and clinical responses to ensure therapeutic effectiveness and minimize toxicity.
   - **Example**: Monitoring INR levels in patients on warfarin therapy to adjust doses and prevent interactions with other medications like NSAIDs.

4. **Alternative Medications**:

   - **Approach**: Substitute one of the interacting drugs with a safer alternative that does not have the same interaction potential.

- **Example**: Replacing a beta-blocker with a calcium channel blocker in a patient who requires a beta-agonist for asthma management.

5. **Dose Adjustment**:

  - **Approach**: Adjust the doses of the interacting medications to minimize adverse effects and ensure therapeutic efficacy.
  - **Example**: Reducing the dose of an antidiabetic drug when a patient is also taking a medication that enhances its effect, like a fibrate, to avoid hypoglycemia.

6. **Scheduling and Timing**:

  - **Approach**: Stagger the administration times of interacting drugs to minimize their interaction potential.
  - **Example**: Taking antacids several hours before or after tetracycline antibiotics to prevent reduced absorption.

Case Studies
Case Study 1: Antagonism in Asthma Management
Problem:

- A patient with asthma and hypertension is prescribed albuterol (a beta-agonist) and propranolol (a non-selective beta-blocker).

Impact:

- The beta-blocker antagonizes the effect of albuterol, leading to poor asthma control and frequent exacerbations.

Management Strategy:

- **Solution**: Substitute propranolol with a selective beta-blocker like metoprolol, which has less interaction with beta-agonists used in asthma.

Outcome:

- Improved asthma control and effective management of hypertension.

Case Study 2: Increased Bleeding Risk with Warfarin and NSAIDs
Problem:

- A patient on warfarin therapy for atrial fibrillation experiences gastrointestinal bleeding after starting an NSAID for arthritis pain.

Impact:

- The combination of warfarin and NSAIDs increases the risk of bleeding due to their additive anticoagulant effects.

Management Strategy:

- **Solution:** Discontinue the NSAID and switch to acetaminophen for pain management. Monitor INR levels closely to maintain therapeutic anticoagulation without increasing bleeding risk.

Outcome:

- Resolution of gastrointestinal bleeding and effective pain management with minimal risk.

Case Study 3: Reduced Antibiotic Efficacy with Antacids
Problem:

- A patient with a bacterial infection shows poor response to tetracycline therapy while taking antacids for heartburn.

Impact:

- The antacids reduce the absorption of tetracycline, leading to subtherapeutic antibiotic levels and persistent infection.

Management Strategy:

- **Solution:** Advise the patient to take tetracycline at least two hours before or after antacids. Consider switching to an alternative antibiotic if necessary.

Outcome:

- Improved antibiotic efficacy and resolution of the infection.

Examples and Case Studies
Real-World Examples of Incompatibilities
Practical Examples from Clinical Practice

1. **Aspirin and Warfarin**:

   - **Example**: Concurrent use of aspirin and warfarin increases the risk of bleeding due to their combined anticoagulant effects.
   - **Clinical Practice**: Patients on warfarin are advised to avoid aspirin unless specifically recommended by their healthcare provider, and regular monitoring of INR (International Normalized Ratio) is essential.

2. **Calcium Supplements and Levothyroxine**:

   - **Example**: Calcium supplements can bind to levothyroxine in the gastrointestinal tract, reducing its absorption and efficacy in treating hypothyroidism.
   - **Clinical Practice**: Patients are instructed to take levothyroxine on an empty stomach, at least four hours apart from calcium supplements.

3. **Antacids and Tetracyclines**:

   - **Example**: Antacids containing aluminum, magnesium, or calcium can form insoluble complexes with tetracyclines, reducing their absorption and therapeutic effect.
   - **Clinical Practice**: Tetracyclines should be taken at least two hours before or after antacids.

Detailed Case Studies
Case Study 1: Antagonism Between Beta-Blockers and Beta-Agonists
Problem:

- A 60-year-old patient with chronic obstructive pulmonary disease (COPD) and hypertension was prescribed albuterol (a beta-agonist) for COPD and propranolol (a non-selective beta-blocker) for hypertension. The patient experienced worsening respiratory symptoms and frequent COPD exacerbations.

Analysis:

- **Mechanism**: Propranolol antagonizes the effects of albuterol by blocking beta-adrenergic receptors, which are essential for bronchodilation.
- **Clinical Significance**: This antagonism reduces the effectiveness of albuterol, leading to poor control of COPD symptoms.

Management Strategy:

- **Solution**: The patient's propranolol was switched to a selective beta-blocker, metoprolol, which has less interaction with beta-agonists.
- **Outcome**: The patient's respiratory symptoms improved, and COPD exacerbations decreased, while hypertension remained well-controlled.

Lessons Learned:

- When prescribing beta-blockers to patients with respiratory conditions, selective beta-blockers are preferable to avoid antagonistic interactions with beta-agonists.
- Regular monitoring and medication review can help identify and manage therapeutic incompatibilities.

Case Study 2: Increased Bleeding Risk with Warfarin and NSAIDs Problem:

- A 45-year-old patient on warfarin therapy for atrial fibrillation developed gastrointestinal bleeding after starting ibuprofen (an NSAID) for chronic back pain.

Analysis:

- **Mechanism**: NSAIDs inhibit platelet aggregation and can cause gastrointestinal irritation, which, when combined with the anticoagulant effects of warfarin, increases the risk of bleeding.
- **Clinical Significance**: The interaction between warfarin and NSAIDs can lead to severe bleeding complications.

Management Strategy:

- **Solution**: Ibuprofen was discontinued, and the patient was prescribed acetaminophen for pain management. INR levels were closely monitored and warfarin dosage adjusted as necessary.
- **Outcome**: The gastrointestinal bleeding resolved, and the patient's pain was effectively managed with acetaminophen.

Lessons Learned:

- Avoiding NSAIDs in patients on warfarin can prevent bleeding complications. Alternatives like acetaminophen should be considered for pain management.
- Close monitoring of INR levels is essential when patients on warfarin are prescribed new medications.

Case Study 3: Reduced Efficacy of Antibiotics with Antacids
Problem:

- A 35 year old patient with a bacterial infection showed poor response to doxycycline therapy while taking antacids for gastroesophageal reflux disease (GERD).

Analysis:

- **Mechanism**: Antacids containing aluminum and magnesium ions form insoluble complexes with doxycycline, reducing its absorption and bioavailability.
- **Clinical Significance**: This interaction can lead to subtherapeutic levels of doxycycline, resulting in ineffective treatment of the infection.

Management Strategy:

- **Solution:** The patient was advised to take doxycycline at least two hours before or after taking antacids. A follow-up antibiotic sensitivity test was performed to confirm the effectiveness of doxycycline against the infection.
- **Outcome:** The patient's infection was successfully treated after adjusting the administration times of doxycycline and antacids.

Lessons Learned:

- Timing the administration of interacting medications can prevent reduced efficacy. Clear patient instructions are crucial for ensuring proper medication use.
- Continuous assessment and adjustment of treatment plans are necessary to manage drug interactions effectively.

Lessons Learned and Best Practices
Insights and Recommendations Based on Case Studies

1. **Comprehensive Medication Review:**

   - Regularly review all medications a patient is taking, including over-the-counter drugs and supplements, to identify potential incompatibilities.

2. **Patient Education:**

   - Educate patients on the importance of timing and proper administration of medications to avoid interactions. Provide clear instructions and explanations.

3. **Therapeutic Drug Monitoring:**

   - Monitor drug levels and clinical parameters (e.g., INR for warfarin) to ensure therapeutic efficacy and safety, especially when new medications are introduced.

4. **Alternative Therapies:**

- Consider alternative medications with less interaction potential when prescribing treatments for patients with complex medical conditions.

5. **Collaborative Care:**

- Encourage collaboration between healthcare providers, including pharmacists, physicians, and nurses, to manage and prevent drug interactions effectively.

6. **Documentation and Reporting:**

- Document any observed incompatibilities and adverse reactions. Report significant interactions to improve understanding and management of therapeutic incompatibilities.

CHAPTER TWELVE

Semisolid Dosage Forms

Semisolid Dosage Forms

Definitions and Classification

Basic Definition of Semisolid Dosage Forms
  Semisolid Dosage Forms:

- **Definition**: Semisolid dosage forms are pharmaceutical preparations with a consistency between solid and liquid. They are intended for external application to the skin or mucous membranes and are designed to exert local or systemic effects. Common examples include ointments, creams, gels, and pastes.

  Explanation of Semisolid Dosage Forms in Pharmacy
Semisolid dosage forms are widely used in pharmacy due to their versatile applications and ability to deliver drugs effectively to specific sites. They provide a medium for the incorporation of active pharmaceutical ingredients (APIs) and excipients, facilitating targeted delivery and controlled release. Their unique properties, such as spreadability, adhesion, and ability to form protective films, make them suitable for various therapeutic purposes.
  Classification of Semisolid Dosage Forms
  1. Ointments
  Definition and Characteristics:

- **Definition**: Ointments are semisolid preparations intended for external application to the skin or mucous membranes. They consist of a single-phase base in which APIs are dissolved or dispersed.
- **Characteristics**: Ointments are generally greasy, occlusive, and provide prolonged contact with the application site. They are typically composed of hydrophobic bases, such as petrolatum, lanolin, or paraffin.

Types of Ointments:

- **Hydrocarbon Bases**: (e.g., petrolatum) Provide an occlusive barrier, preventing water loss and enhancing hydration of the skin.
- **Absorption Bases**: (e.g., hydrophilic petrolatum) Allow the incorporation of aqueous solutions, forming w/o emulsions.
- **Water-Removable Bases**: (e.g., vanishing creams) Easily washed off with water, forming o/w emulsions.
- **Water-Soluble Bases**: (e.g., polyethylene glycol ointment) Non-greasy and easily washable with water.

2. Creams
Types and Properties:

- **Definition**: Creams are semisolid emulsions containing one or more APIs. They can be water-in-oil (w/o) or oil-in-water (o/w) emulsions, depending on the composition of the internal and external phases.
- **Properties**: Creams are less greasy than ointments, spread easily, and are well absorbed by the skin. They provide a cooling effect upon application due to water evaporation.

Types of Creams:

- **Oil-in-Water (o/w) Creams**: Non-greasy, easily washed off with water, and suitable for moisturizing and hydrating the skin. Commonly used for cosmetic and medicinal purposes.
- **Water-in-Oil (w/o) Creams**: Greasier and more emollient, providing a protective barrier and preventing water loss. Ideal for dry and sensitive skin conditions.

3. Gels

Definition and Uses:

- **Definition**: Gels are semisolid systems consisting of a liquid phase (usually water) thickened with a gelling agent to form a three-dimensional matrix. They can be hydrophilic (hydrogels) or hydrophobic (organogels).
- **Uses**: Gels are used for their cooling effect, ease of application, and quick absorption. They are suitable for delivering both hydrophilic and lipophilic drugs. Common applications include topical analgesics, anti-inflammatory agents, and cosmetic products.

Types of Gels:

- **Hydrogels**: Water-based gels, providing a cooling effect and hydration. Used for burns, wounds, and as drug delivery systems.
- **Organogels**: Oil-based gels, providing a protective and occlusive layer. Used for topical delivery of lipophilic drugs.

4. Pastes

Characteristics and Applications:

- **Definition**: Pastes are thick, semisolid preparations containing a high concentration of finely powdered substances (e.g., zinc oxide, starch) dispersed in an ointment base. They are stiffer and less greasy than ointments.
- **Characteristics**: Pastes adhere well to the skin, providing a protective barrier and remaining in place for extended periods. They are less occlusive than ointments but provide good absorption of exudates.
- **Applications**: Used in conditions requiring protective, astringent, or antiseptic effects. Commonly used for diaper rash, eczema, and other inflammatory skin conditions.

Mechanisms and Factors Influencing Dermal Penetration

Mechanisms of Dermal Penetration
  Diffusion
  Process and Significance:

- **Process**: Diffusion is the primary mechanism by which drugs penetrate the skin. It involves the movement of drug molecules from an area of higher concentration (the surface of the skin) to an area of lower concentration (within the skin layers). This passive process is driven by the concentration gradient and does not require energy.
- **Significance**: The rate of diffusion determines the speed and extent of drug absorption through the skin. It is crucial for the effectiveness of topical and transdermal drug delivery systems. The stratum corneum, the outermost layer of the skin, acts as a barrier to diffusion, and the drug must pass through this layer to reach the viable epidermis and dermis.

Partition Coefficient
Role in Dermal Absorption:

- **Definition**: The partition coefficient (log P) is a measure of a drug's lipophilicity, indicating its ability to partition between lipophilic (oil) and hydrophilic (water) environments.
- **Role**: A drug's partition coefficient influences its ability to penetrate the skin. Drugs with moderate lipophilicity (log P values between 1 and 3) are ideal for dermal absorption, as they can partition into both the lipid-rich stratum corneum and the aqueous environment of the deeper skin layers. Highly lipophilic drugs may remain in the stratum corneum, while highly hydrophilic drugs may not effectively penetrate the skin barrier.

Factors Influencing Penetration
Skin Condition
Impact of Skin Health and Integrity:

- **Healthy Skin**: Intact, healthy skin provides a robust barrier to drug penetration. The stratum corneum's lipid matrix and tightly packed keratinocytes prevent excessive drug absorption.
- **Damaged or Diseased Skin**: Conditions like eczema, psoriasis, or wounds disrupt the skin barrier, increasing permeability and enhancing drug penetration. This can lead to higher local and systemic drug absorption, potentially resulting in increased efficacy or adverse effects.
- **Hydration**: Hydrated skin has increased permeability due to the swelling of the stratum corneum, which can enhance drug absorption.

Formulation Factors
Ingredients and Formulation Effects:

- **Base Composition**: The choice of base (ointment, cream, gel) affects drug release and penetration. For example, ointments (hydrophobic bases) provide occlusion, enhancing drug penetration by hydrating the stratum corneum.
- **Penetration Enhancers**: Ingredients like alcohols, fatty acids, and surfactants can disrupt the lipid structure of the stratum corneum, increasing drug permeability. For example, ethanol is commonly used to enhance the penetration of topical corticosteroids.
- **pH**: The pH of the formulation can influence drug ionization and, consequently, its penetration. Drugs are better absorbed in their non-ionized form.

Application Method
Techniques and Their Influence on Penetration:

- **Occlusion**: Covering the application site with an occlusive dressing (e.g., plastic wrap) increases drug penetration by hydrating the stratum corneum and increasing skin temperature.
- **Massage**: Rubbing or massaging the formulation into the skin can enhance drug penetration by increasing local blood flow and promoting drug diffusion.
- **Application Frequency and Dose**: Frequent application and higher doses increase the concentration gradient, driving more drug into the skin. However, this must be balanced with the risk of local and systemic side effects.
- **Surface Area**: Applying the drug to a larger surface area increases the total amount of drug absorbed, which can be important for systemic effects.

Preparation of Semisolid Dosage Forms

Ointments

Types of Ointments
Classification Based on Bases:

1. **Hydrocarbon (Oleaginous) Bases:**

   - **Examples**: Petrolatum, White petrolatum, Mineral oil
   - **Characteristics**: Greasy, occlusive, provides an emollient effect, and prevents water loss by forming a barrier on the skin.

1. **Absorption Bases:**

   - **Examples**: Hydrophilic petrolatum, Anhydrous lanolin, Aquaphor
   - **Characteristics**: Can absorb water and form w/o emulsions, more hydrating than hydrocarbon bases, suitable for incorporating aqueous solutions.

3. **Water-Removable Bases:**

   - **Examples**: Hydrophilic ointment, Vanishing cream, Cetomacrogol cream
   - **Characteristics**: O/W emulsions, non-greasy, easily washed off with water, provides a cooling effect upon application.

4. **Water-Soluble Bases:**

   - **Examples**: Polyethylene glycol (PEG) ointment
   - **Characteristics**: Completely water-soluble, non-greasy, easy to wash off, suitable for drugs that need to be absorbed quickly.

Formulation Techniques
Step-by-Step Preparation Methods:

1. **Incorporation Method:**

   - **Step 1: Weighing and Measuring**: Accurately weigh the API and base components.
   - **Step 2: Mixing**: Mix the API with a portion of the base using a mortar and pestle to form a smooth paste.

- **Step 3: Incorporation**: Gradually incorporate the rest of the base into the paste until uniform.
- **Step 4: Homogenization**: Use an ointment mill or homogenizer for even distribution and to remove any lumps.
- **Step 5: Packaging**: Transfer the ointment into suitable containers, ensuring no air pockets remain.

2. **Fusion Method:**

- **Step 1: Weighing and Measuring**: Accurately weigh the base components and API.
- **Step 2: Melting**: Melt the base components with higher melting points in a water bath.
- **Step 3: Mixing**: Add the API and other heat-stable components to the melted base, stirring continuously.
- **Step 4: Cooling**: Allow the mixture to cool while stirring until it reaches a semi-solid state.
- **Step 5: Homogenization**: If necessary, use an ointment mill or homogenizer to ensure uniform consistency.
- **Step 6: Packaging**: Transfer the prepared ointment into containers, ensuring even filling and no air pockets.

Common Ingredients
Essential Components and Their Roles:

1. **Active Pharmaceutical Ingredient (API):**

- **Role**: Provides the therapeutic effect. The choice of API depends on the condition being treated (e.g., anti-inflammatory, antifungal, antibacterial).

2. **Base:**

- **Role**: The vehicle that carries the API, affecting the ointment's consistency, occlusiveness, and absorption. Types of bases include hydrocarbon, absorption, water-removable, and water-soluble bases.

3. **Emulsifying Agents:**

- **Role**: Help in the formation and stabilization of emulsions, ensuring uniform distribution of ingredients. Examples include Span, Tween, and cetyl alcohol.

4. **Humectants**:

- **Role**: Attract and retain moisture, keeping the skin hydrated. Common humectants include glycerin, propylene glycol, and sorbitol.

5. **Preservatives**:

- **Role**: Prevent microbial growth and extend the shelf life of the ointment. Examples include methylparaben, propylparaben, and benzalkonium chloride.

6. **Antioxidants**:

- **Role**: Prevent oxidation of the API and base, maintaining the efficacy and stability of the ointment. Common antioxidants include butylated hydroxytoluene (BHT) and butylated hydroxyanisole (BHA).

7. **Stabilizers**:

- **Role**: Enhance the physical and chemical stability of the ointment. Examples include sodium citrate and citric acid for pH adjustment.

Example Formulation:
Hydrocarbon-Based Ointment (Petrolatum Base):

- **Ingredients**:

  - Active Ingredient: 1% Hydrocortisone
  - Base: White petrolatum
  - Emulsifying Agent: Span 60 (if needed for additional stability)
  - Preservative: Methylparaben (if needed for additional stability)

Preparation:

1. Weigh the required amount of hydrocortisone and white petrolatum.
2. Melt the white petrolatum in a water bath if needed.
3. Disperse the hydrocortisone in a small portion of the melted petrolatum until a smooth paste is formed.
4. Gradually incorporate the rest of the melted petrolatum into the paste.
5. Homogenize the mixture using an ointment mill to ensure even distribution.
6. Cool the mixture while stirring continuously.
7. Package the ointment into appropriate containers, ensuring no air pockets.

The preparation of ointments involves selecting appropriate types based on the desired therapeutic effect and characteristics. Formulation techniques like the incorporation and fusion methods ensure uniform distribution of the API and other ingredients. Understanding the roles of common ingredients helps in designing effective and stable ointment formulations for various clinical applications.

Pastes

Definition and Characteristics
Definition:

- **Pastes:** Pastes are thick, semisolid preparations that contain a high concentration of finely powdered substances dispersed in an ointment base. They have a stiffer consistency compared to ointments and creams due to the presence of a significant amount of solid particles.

Characteristics:

- **High Viscosity:** Due to the high content of solid particles, pastes are more viscous and less greasy than ointments.
- **Adhesiveness:** They adhere well to the skin and form a protective barrier, making them suitable for localized applications.
- **Opacity:** Pastes are generally opaque and provide a physical barrier on the skin, protecting it from environmental factors.
- **Reduced Absorption:** The high solid content reduces the penetration of active ingredients into the skin, providing more localized action.

Properties and Uses
Properties:

- **Non-Greasy**: Unlike ointments, pastes have a non-greasy texture due to the high concentration of solids.
- **Protective Barrier**: They provide a protective coating on the skin, shielding it from irritants and moisture.
- **Absorbent**: Pastes can absorb secretions and moisture, making them suitable for wet or weeping skin conditions.

Uses:

- **Protective**: Used to protect irritated or inflamed skin from further damage.
- **Astringent**: Provide a drying effect, useful in treating weeping skin conditions.
- **Anti-Inflammatory**: Used to deliver anti-inflammatory agents to localized areas of inflammation.

Preparation Methods
Techniques for Formulation:

1. **Incorporation Method:**

   - **Step 1: Weighing**: Accurately weigh the solid powders (e.g., zinc oxide, starch) and the ointment base.
   - **Step 2: Mixing**: Gradually add the powdered solids to the ointment base while continuously mixing to form a smooth paste.
   - **Step 3: Homogenization**: Use a spatula or mechanical mixer to ensure even distribution of the solid particles throughout the base.
   - **Step 4: Adjustment**: Adjust the consistency by adding more base or powders as needed to achieve the desired thickness.
   - **Step 5: Packaging**: Transfer the paste into appropriate containers, ensuring even filling and no air pockets.

2. **Fusion Method** (for heat-stable ingredients):

- **Step 1**: **Weighing**: Accurately weigh the solid powders and the ointment base.
- **Step 2**: **Melting**: Melt the ointment base in a water bath if it is solid at room temperature.
- **Step 3**: **Incorporation**: Gradually add the solid powders to the melted base while stirring continuously.
- **Step 4**: **Cooling**: Allow the mixture to cool while stirring until it reaches a semi-solid state.
- **Step 5**: **Homogenization**: Ensure uniform distribution of the powders using a spatula or mechanical mixer.
- **Step 6**: **Packaging**: Transfer the paste into containers before it completely solidifies.

Applications and Uses
Therapeutic Uses:

1. **Diaper Rash**: Zinc oxide paste is commonly used to protect and heal diaper rash by forming a barrier and reducing irritation.
2. **Psoriasis**: Coal tar paste is used to reduce scaling and inflammation in psoriasis patients.
3. **Eczema**: Topical corticosteroid pastes provide anti-inflammatory effects for localized eczema flare-ups.
4. **Burns and Wounds**: Antimicrobial pastes (e.g., silver sulfadiazine) are used to prevent infection and promote healing in burns and wounds.

Cosmetic Uses:

1. **Face Masks**: Pastes containing clays and other absorbent materials are used in cosmetic face masks to cleanse and tighten the skin.
2. **Exfoliants**: Abrasive pastes containing fine particles are used as exfoliants to remove dead skin cells and improve skin texture.
3. **Anti-Acne Treatments**: Medicated pastes with ingredients like sulfur or salicylic acid are used to treat acne by reducing inflammation and absorbing excess oil.

Example Formulation:
Zinc Oxide Paste for Diaper Rash:

- **Ingredients**:

  - Zinc oxide: 20%
  - Starch: 10%
  - White petrolatum: 70%

Preparation:

1. Weigh the zinc oxide, starch, and white petrolatum accurately.
2. Gradually add the zinc oxide and starch to the white petrolatum while mixing continuously to form a smooth, uniform paste.
3. Ensure thorough mixing to avoid any lumps or uneven distribution of the powders.
4. Transfer the prepared paste into suitable containers, such as tubes or jars, and label appropriately.

Pastes are versatile semisolid dosage forms with unique properties that make them suitable for various therapeutic and cosmetic applications. Their high viscosity, protective barrier, and non-greasy texture offer distinct advantages over other semisolid forms like ointments and creams. Understanding the preparation methods and common ingredients allows for the effective formulation of pastes tailored to specific clinical needs, ensuring optimal therapeutic outcomes and patient satisfaction.

Creams

Types of Creams (Oil-in-Water, Water-in-Oil)
  Oil-in-Water (O/W) Creams
  Characteristics:

- **Appearance and Texture**: O/W creams are generally lighter, less greasy, and have a smooth, creamy texture.
- **Water Content**: They have a higher water content, which makes them easier to wash off with water.
- **Cooling Effect**: These creams provide a cooling effect upon application as the water content evaporates.
- **Applications**: Commonly used as moisturizers, cosmetic creams, and for delivering hydrophilic drugs.

Water-in-Oil (W/O) Creams
Characteristics:

- **Appearance and Texture**: W/O creams are greasier, thicker, and more emollient compared to O/W creams.
- **Oil Content**: They contain a higher oil content, which provides a more occlusive layer that prevents water loss from the skin.
- **Longer Hydration**: These creams are better for prolonged hydration and are more suitable for dry or sensitive skin.
- **Applications**: Commonly used for treating dry skin conditions, as barrier creams, and for delivering lipophilic drugs.

Differences:

- **Composition**: O/W creams have water as the continuous phase and oil as the dispersed phase, while W/O creams have oil as the continuous phase and water as the dispersed phase.
- **Feel and Usage**: O/W creams are lighter and more suited for daytime use, whereas W/O creams are heavier and better for nighttime use or for treating very dry skin.

Preparation Techniques
Methods and Equipment Used
1. Oil-in-Water (O/W) Creams
Method:

- **Step 1: Weighing Ingredients**: Accurately weigh the oil phase components (oils, emulsifiers) and water phase components (water, preservatives).
- **Step 2: Heating**: Heat the oil phase and water phase separately to about 70-75°C to ensure proper melting and mixing of ingredients.
- **Step 3: Mixing**: Slowly add the oil phase to the water phase while stirring continuously using a high-shear mixer or homogenizer.
- **Step 4: Cooling**: Continue mixing and gradually cool the mixture to room temperature to form a stable emulsion.
- **Step 5: Packaging**: Once the cream has cooled and achieved the desired consistency, transfer it to suitable containers.

Equipment:

- **Hot Plates**: For heating the oil and water phases.
- **High-Shear Mixers or Homogenizers**: For creating a stable emulsion.
- **Stirring Rods and Thermometers**: For continuous stirring and temperature monitoring.

2. Water-in-Oil (W/O) Creams
Method:

- **Step 1: Weighing Ingredients**: Accurately weigh the oil phase components (oils, emulsifiers) and water phase components (water, preservatives).
- **Step 2: Heating**: Heat the oil phase and water phase separately to about 70-75°C.
- **Step 3: Mixing**: Slowly add the water phase to the oil phase while stirring continuously using a high-shear mixer or homogenizer.
- **Step 4: Cooling**: Continue mixing and gradually cool the mixture to room temperature to form a stable emulsion.
- **Step 5: Packaging**: Once the cream has cooled and achieved the desired consistency, transfer it to suitable containers.

Equipment:

- **Hot Plates**: For heating the oil and water phases.
- **High-Shear Mixers or Homogenizers**: For creating a stable emulsion.
- **Stirring Rods and Thermometers**: For continuous stirring and temperature monitoring.

Stabilization Methods
Techniques to Ensure Product Stability

1. **Use of Emulsifiers:**

   - **Function**: Emulsifiers stabilize the emulsion by reducing the surface tension between the oil and water phases.
   - **Examples**: Polysorbates (Tween), sorbitan esters (Span), and cetyl alcohol.

2. **Phase Inversion Temperature (PIT):**

- **Technique**: By controlling the temperature at which the emulsion inverts from O/W to W/O or vice versa, the stability of the emulsion can be optimized.
- **Application**: Adjusting the formulation to achieve a PIT near room temperature for better stability.

3. **pH Adjustment:**

- **Function**: Maintaining the pH of the cream within a specific range to ensure the stability of both the emulsion and the active ingredients.
- **Examples**: Using buffers such as citric acid or sodium citrate to maintain the desired pH.

4. **Antioxidants:**

- **Function**: Prevent oxidation of the oil phase, which can cause rancidity and destabilize the emulsion.
- **Examples**: Butylated hydroxytoluene (BHT), tocopherols (vitamin E).

5. **Preservatives:**

- **Function**: Prevent microbial growth in the cream, ensuring its safety and longevity.
- **Examples**: Parabens (methylparaben, propylparaben), benzyl alcohol.

6. **Thickeners and Gelling Agents:**

- **Function**: Increase the viscosity of the cream, providing better stability and texture.
- **Examples**: Carbomers, xanthan gum, hydroxyethyl cellulose.

7. **Homogenization:**

- **Technique**: Using high-shear mixers or homogenizers to create a uniform and stable emulsion with small droplet sizes.
- **Benefit**: Smaller droplet sizes result in a more stable emulsion and improved texture.

Example Formulation:
Oil-in-Water (O/W) Moisturizing Cream:

- Ingredients:

  - Oil Phase: Cetyl alcohol, stearic acid, mineral oil, emulsifying wax
  - Water Phase: Distilled water, glycerin, preservative (e.g., methylparaben)
  - Active Ingredient: Vitamin E (tocopherol)

Preparation:

1. Weigh the oil phase and water phase components separately.
2. Heat both phases to 70-75°C.
3. Slowly add the oil phase to the water phase while continuously stirring with a high-shear mixer.
4. Gradually cool the mixture while stirring until it reaches room temperature.
5. Add the active ingredient (vitamin E) during the cooling process.
6. Transfer the cream to containers and label appropriately.

Gels

Types of Gels (Hydrogels, Organogels)
Definitions and Examples
Hydrogels:

- **Definition**: Hydrogels are three-dimensional, hydrophilic polymer networks that can absorb and retain large amounts of water while maintaining their structure.
- **Examples**: Carbomer gels, polyvinyl alcohol (PVA) gels, and gelatin gels.

- **Properties**: They are typically transparent, non-greasy, and provide a cooling sensation upon application. Hydrogels can swell in water and are often used for their moisturizing properties.

Organogels:

- **Definition**: Organogels are semi-solid systems composed of a liquid organic phase (such as an oil) immobilized by a three-dimensional network of a gelator.
- **Examples**: Lecithin organogels, pluronic organogels.
- **Properties**: They can be greasy or non-greasy depending on the oil used. Organogels are used for their ability to incorporate lipophilic drugs and provide a controlled release of active ingredients.

Preparation Methods
Steps Involved in Formulation
Hydrogels:
Step 1: Weighing and Dissolving Polymers:

- Accurately weigh the polymer (e.g., carbomer) and other ingredients.
- Dissolve the polymer in distilled water, often requiring gentle heating and stirring to ensure complete dissolution.

Step 2: Neutralization (if required):

- For polymers like carbomer, neutralize the solution by adding a neutralizing agent (e.g., triethanolamine) slowly while stirring. This step helps the gel to form and thicken.

Step 3: Incorporation of Active Ingredients:

- Dissolve or disperse the active pharmaceutical ingredient (API) in the gel base, ensuring uniform distribution.

Step 4: pH Adjustment:

- Adjust the pH of the gel to the desired level using suitable buffers or acids/bases.

Step 5: Homogenization and Deaeration:

- Homogenize the gel to ensure even consistency and remove any air bubbles by letting it stand or using a vacuum deaerator.

Step 6: Packaging:

- Transfer the prepared hydrogel into suitable containers and label appropriately.

Organogels:
Step 1: Weighing and Mixing Components:

- Accurately weigh the oil phase (e.g., lecithin) and the gelator.

Step 2: Heating and Mixing:

- Heat the oil phase gently to dissolve the gelator completely while stirring continuously.

Step 3: Cooling and Gel Formation:

- Allow the mixture to cool to room temperature or lower to facilitate gel formation.

Step 4: Incorporation of Active Ingredients:

- Add the API to the cooled gel, ensuring even distribution by mixing thoroughly.

Step 5: Homogenization and Deaeration:

- Homogenize the organogel to achieve uniform consistency and remove air bubbles.

Step 6: Packaging:

- Transfer the organogel into appropriate containers and label them.

Examples and Uses
Specific Applications and Case Studies
Hydrogels:
Example 1: Carbomer Gel for Topical Drug Delivery
Ingredients:

- Carbomer: 1%
- Distilled water: 98%
- Triethanolamine: 1%
- API: 0.5% (e.g., lidocaine)

Preparation:

1. Dissolve carbomer in distilled water with continuous stirring until fully hydrated.
2. Neutralize the solution with triethanolamine to form a gel.
3. Dissolve the API in the gel with thorough mixing.
4. Adjust the pH if necessary.
5. Homogenize and remove air bubbles.
6. Package the gel in tubes or jars.

Uses:

- Local anesthetic gel for pain relief in minor cuts, burns, or insect bites.

Example 2: Polyvinyl Alcohol (PVA) Hydrogel for Wound Dressing
Ingredients:

- PVA: 10%
- Distilled water: 90%
- Glycerin: 5%
- Antimicrobial agent: 0.5% (e.g., chlorhexidine)

Preparation:

1. Dissolve PVA and glycerin in distilled water by heating and stirring.
2. Add the antimicrobial agent and mix thoroughly.
3. Pour the solution into molds and allow it to cool and form a gel.

4. Remove air bubbles and package.

Uses:

- Hydrating wound dressings that provide a moist environment for wound healing and deliver antimicrobial agents to prevent infection.

Organogels:
Example 1: Lecithin Organogel for Transdermal Drug Delivery
Ingredients:

- Lecithin: 5%
- Isopropyl palmitate: 90%
- Sorbitan monostearate: 3%
- API: 2% (e.g., diclofenac)

Preparation:

1. Heat lecithin, isopropyl palmitate, and sorbitan monostearate together until dissolved.
2. Allow the mixture to cool to form the organogel.
3. Incorporate the API with thorough mixing.
4. Homogenize and remove air bubbles.
5. Package the organogel in suitable containers.

Uses:

- Transdermal delivery of anti-inflammatory drugs for chronic pain management.

Example 2: Pluronic Organogel for Controlled Drug Release
Ingredients:

- Pluronic F127: 20%
- Distilled water: 80%
- API: 1% (e.g., ibuprofen)

Preparation:

1. Dissolve pluronic F127 in cold distilled water with continuous stirring.
2. Add the API and mix until fully dissolved.
3. Allow the solution to gel at room temperature.
4. Homogenize and remove air bubbles.
5. Package the organogel in tubes or jars.

Uses:

- Controlled release gel for anti-inflammatory and analgesic effects.

Excipients Used in Semisolid Dosage Forms

Types of Excipients
    Emulsifying Agents
    Role and Examples:

- **Role**: Emulsifying agents stabilize emulsions by reducing the surface tension between the oil and water phases, preventing separation. They help form and maintain a uniform dispersion of one liquid in another.
- **Examples**:

  - **Non-ionic emulsifiers**: Polysorbates (e.g., Tween 80), sorbitan esters (e.g., Span 60)
  - **Anionic emulsifiers**: Sodium lauryl sulfate, sodium stearate
  - **Cationic emulsifiers**: Cetyltrimethylammonium bromide
  - **Natural emulsifiers**: Lecithin, acacia gum

Stabilizers
Types and Importance:

- **Role**: Stabilizers enhance the physical and chemical stability of semisolid dosage forms by preventing phase separation, sedimentation, and degradation of active ingredients.
- **Types and Examples**:

  - **Antioxidants**: Prevent oxidation of the formulation. Examples: Butylated hydroxytoluene (BHT), tocopherols (vitamin E)

- **Chelating agents**: Bind metal ions that catalyze degradation reactions. Examples: Ethylenediaminetetraacetic acid (EDTA), citric acid
- **Buffering agents**: Maintain the pH of the formulation to ensure stability. Examples: Sodium citrate, phosphate buffers

Preservatives
Common Preservatives Used:

- **Role**: Preservatives prevent microbial growth in semisolid dosage forms, ensuring the safety and longevity of the product.
- **Examples**:

  - **Parabens**: Methylparaben, propylparaben
  - **Alcohols**: Benzyl alcohol, phenoxyethanol
  - **Quaternary ammonium compounds**: Benzalkonium chloride
  - **Organic acids**: Sorbic acid, benzoic acid

Humectants
Function and Examples:

- **Role**: Humectants attract and retain moisture in the formulation, helping to keep the product hydrated and enhancing skin moisturization.
- **Examples**:

  - **Glycerin**: Widely used for its excellent humectant properties
  - **Propylene glycol**: Effective humectant and solvent
  - **Sorbitol**: Commonly used in moisturizing formulations
  - **Urea**: Adds moisture and has keratolytic properties

Viscosity Enhancers
Impact on Product Consistency:

- **Role**: Viscosity enhancers increase the thickness and improve the consistency of semisolid dosage forms, ensuring the product remains stable and easy to apply.
- **Examples**:

- **Polymers**: Carbomers (e.g., Carbopol), hydroxyethyl cellulose, xanthan gum
- **Natural Gums**: Guar gum, acacia gum, tragacanth
- **Clays**: Bentonite, hectorite

Example Formulation Components:
Example 1: Moisturizing Cream (Oil-in-Water Emulsion)

- **Emulsifying Agents**: Polysorbate 60, sorbitan stearate
- **Stabilizers**: Butylated hydroxytoluene (BHT), EDTA, sodium citrate
- **Preservatives**: Methylparaben, propylparaben
- **Humectants**: Glycerin, propylene glycol
- **Viscosity Enhancers**: Carbomer, xanthan gum

Preparation:

1. **Weighing**: Accurately weigh all the ingredients.
2. **Heating**: Heat the oil phase (containing emulsifying agents, stabilizers, and oils) and the water phase (containing humectants and water) separately to 70-75°C.
3. **Mixing**: Slowly add the oil phase to the water phase while stirring continuously to form an emulsion.
4. **Cooling**: Gradually cool the mixture while stirring to maintain a uniform consistency.
5. **Addition of Preservatives**: Add preservatives and adjust the pH as needed.
6. **Homogenization**: Homogenize the mixture to ensure even distribution of all components.
7. **Packaging**: Transfer the prepared cream into suitable containers and label them.

Role of Excipients
Enhancing Stability
Methods to Improve Product Lifespan:

1. **Antioxidants:**

- **Function**: Antioxidants prevent the oxidation of active ingredients and excipients, thereby prolonging the shelf life of the product.
- **Examples**: Butylated hydroxytoluene (BHT), tocopherols (vitamin E).
- **Method**: Incorporate antioxidants into formulations containing susceptible ingredients like oils or unsaturated fatty acids to prevent rancidity and degradation.

2. **Chelating Agents**:

- **Function**: Chelating agents bind to metal ions that can catalyze degradation reactions, thus enhancing stability.
- **Examples**: Ethylenediaminetetraacetic acid (EDTA), citric acid.
- **Method**: Add chelating agents to formulations to sequester metal ions and prevent oxidative degradation of both active ingredients and excipients.

3. **Preservatives**:

- **Function**: Preservatives inhibit the growth of microorganisms, ensuring the microbiological stability of the product.
- **Examples**: Parabens (methylparaben, propylparaben), benzyl alcohol, phenoxyethanol.
- **Method**: Incorporate preservatives into formulations to protect against contamination during storage and use.

4. **Buffering Agents**:

- **Function**: Buffering agents maintain the pH of the formulation within a stable range, preventing pH-dependent degradation of active ingredients.
- **Examples**: Sodium citrate, phosphate buffers.
- **Method**: Use buffers to stabilize the pH and enhance the chemical stability of the product, especially for pH-sensitive ingredients.

5. **Thickeners and Gelling Agents**:

- **Function**: These agents increase the viscosity of formulations, preventing phase separation and sedimentation of suspended particles.
- **Examples**: Carbomers, xanthan gum, bentonite.
- **Method**: Add thickeners to ensure a consistent texture and stability over the product's lifespan.

Improving Efficacy
How Excipients Enhance Therapeutic Effects:

1. **Enhancers of Drug Penetration and Absorption:**

   - **Function**: Certain excipients enhance the penetration and absorption of active ingredients through the skin or mucous membranes.
   - **Examples**: Ethanol, propylene glycol, dimethyl sulfoxide (DMSO).
   - **Method**: Incorporate penetration enhancers into formulations to improve the bioavailability of the active ingredient, especially in topical and transdermal products.

2. **Bioadhesive Polymers:**

   - **Function**: Bioadhesive polymers increase the residence time of formulations at the site of application, enhancing drug absorption and efficacy.
   - **Examples**: Carbopol, hydroxypropyl methylcellulose (HPMC).
   - **Method**: Use bioadhesive polymers in formulations to prolong contact with the mucosal surfaces, improving the therapeutic effect of the active ingredient.

3. **Solubilizers and Surfactants:**

   - **Function**: Solubilizers and surfactants improve the solubility and dispersion of poorly soluble active ingredients, enhancing their efficacy.
   - **Examples**: Polysorbates (e.g., Tween 80), sodium lauryl sulfate.
   - **Method**: Add solubilizers to formulations to increase the dissolution rate and bioavailability of hydrophobic drugs.

4. pH Adjusters:

- **Function**: pH adjusters optimize the pH for maximum drug stability and absorption.
- **Examples**: Citric acid, sodium hydroxide.
- **Method**: Adjust the pH of formulations to the optimal range for the stability and absorption of the active ingredient.

Ensuring Patient Compliance
Making Products More Acceptable to Users:

1. Humectants:

- **Function**: Humectants retain moisture in the formulation, enhancing skin hydration and making the product more pleasant to use.
- **Examples**: Glycerin, propylene glycol, sorbitol.
- **Method**: Include humectants in formulations to improve skin feel and prevent drying, increasing patient compliance with topical treatments.

2. Emollients:

- **Function**: Emollients soften and smooth the skin, making the product more comfortable to apply and wear.
- **Examples**: Petrolatum, lanolin, mineral oil.
- **Method**: Add emollients to formulations to enhance the sensory properties and acceptability of creams and ointments.

3. Flavoring Agents:

- **Function**: Flavoring agents mask unpleasant tastes in oral formulations, making them more palatable.
- **Examples**: Mint, cherry, citrus flavors.
- **Method**: Incorporate flavoring agents into oral formulations to improve taste and encourage adherence to medication regimens.

4. Coloring Agents:

- **Function**: Coloring agents improve the aesthetic appeal of formulations, making them more visually appealing and acceptable to patients.
- **Examples**: FD&C dyes, iron oxides.
- **Method**: Use appropriate coloring agents to enhance the appearance of the product, particularly in pediatric and cosmetic formulations.

5. **Texturizers**:

- **Function**: Texturizers modify the feel of the product, making it more pleasant to apply and use.
- **Examples**: Silicones, dimethicone, and microcrystalline wax.
- **Method**: Add texturizers to formulations to improve the spreadability and tactile sensation, enhancing user experience and compliance.

Evaluation of Semisolid Dosage Forms

Parameters and Techniques
   Physical Parameters (Viscosity, Spreadability)
   Viscosity
   Methods to Measure and Importance:

- **Measurement Methods**:

- **Brookfield Viscometer**: Measures the torque required to rotate a spindle at a constant speed in the semisolid sample. The viscosity is directly related to the torque needed.
- **Capillary Viscometer**: Measures the time it takes for the semisolid to flow through a capillary tube under gravity or applied pressure.
- **Cone and Plate Viscometer**: Uses a cone-shaped spindle that rotates on a flat plate; the resistance to rotation provides a measure of viscosity.

- **Importance**: Viscosity affects the application and spreadability of semisolid dosage forms. It ensures consistency in product performance, influencing the ease of application, patient comfort, and drug release.

Spreadability
Methods to Measure and Importance:

- **Measurement Methods:**

  - **Parallel Plate Method**: Measures the diameter of a circle formed when a fixed amount of semisolid is placed between two glass plates and a weight is applied for a specified time
  - **Texture Analyzer**: Measures the force required to spread the semisolid sample between two surfaces.

- **Importance**: Spreadability determines how easily the product can be applied to the skin or mucosal surfaces. It influences patient satisfaction and compliance by ensuring even coverage and appropriate dosing.

Chemical Parameters (pH, Homogeneity)
pH
Testing Techniques and Significance:

- **Measurement Methods:**

  - **pH Meter**: A calibrated pH meter is used to measure the pH of the semisolid directly or after dilution with water.

- **Significance**: The pH of semisolid dosage forms should be compatible with the skin or mucous membranes to avoid irritation. It also affects the stability and solubility of the active ingredients.

Homogeneity
Testing Techniques and Significance:

- **Measurement Methods:**

  - **Visual Inspection**: Assessing the uniformity of the product by checking for phase separation, air bubbles, and particle distribution.
  - **Microscopic Examination**: Evaluating the distribution of active ingredients and excipients at the microscopic level to ensure uniformity.

- **Significance**: Homogeneity ensures that each dose of the product contains an equal amount of the active ingredient, providing consistent therapeutic effects and safety.

Microbial Testing (Sterility, Preservation Efficacy)
Sterility
Ensuring Safety and Effectiveness:

- **Testing Techniques**:

  - **Sterility Testing**: Involves incubating the semisolid product in a culture medium to check for the presence of microbial contamination. Common methods include direct inoculation and membrane filtration.

- **Significance**: Sterility testing is crucial for products intended for application to open wounds or sensitive areas to prevent infections.

Preservation Efficacy
Ensuring Safety and Effectiveness:

- **Testing Techniques**:

  - **Preservative Efficacy Testing (PET)**: Also known as antimicrobial effectiveness testing, it involves inoculating the product with known strains of microorganisms and assessing the preservative's ability to inhibit their growth over time.

- **Significance**: Ensures that the preservative system in the formulation is effective in preventing microbial growth, thus ensuring the product's safety and extending its shelf life.

Clinical Evaluation (Efficacy, Irritation Testing)
Efficacy
Assessing Clinical Performance and Patient Safety:

- **Testing Techniques**:

- **In Vivo Studies**: Clinical trials and studies on human subjects to assess the therapeutic effects of the semisolid product.
- **Bioavailability Studies**: Measuring the concentration of the active ingredient in biological fluids to determine the extent and rate of absorption.

- **Significance**: Clinical efficacy testing ensures that the product delivers the intended therapeutic benefits to patients.

Irritation Testing
Assessing Clinical Performance and Patient Safety:

- **Testing Techniques**:

  - **Patch Test**: A small amount of the product is applied to the skin under an occlusive patch for a specified period, and the site is observed for signs of irritation or allergic reactions.
  - **Animal Studies**: Using animal models to predict irritation potential in humans.

- **Significance**: Irritation testing ensures that the product is safe for use and does not cause adverse reactions such as redness, itching, or dermatitis.